"This review of major voices in the discussion of a timely topic provides the reader with valuable perspectives to consider the question. Everyone interested in the theological issue of the violence of the biblical God, especially in the wars with the Canaanites, will benefit by reading this work."

— **Richard S. Hess**
Denver Seminary

"This is a learned and thoughtful discussion. In an area where there is usually much heat Trimm increases the light."

— **R. W. L. Moberly**
Durham University

"Drawing on his expertise on warfare in the ancient Near East, Trimm outlines and critiques common approaches to this vexing ethical issue and considers their implications. Trimm does not offer a solution to the problem. Instead, he astutely lays the groundwork for a robust classroom discussion in which students can wrestle with the issues and develop their own approach to the problem of violence in the Old Testament."

— **Carmen Joy Imes**
Biola University

"This excellent volume takes an honest, hard look at the ways in which biblical scholars have tried to explain the moral challenge posed by the stories of the conquest of Canaan in the Bible. No easy solutions are offered, but the reader will come away with a far better grasp of the nature of the problem."

— **Gary A. Anderson**
University of Notre Dame

"If you are overwhelmed not only by the ethically problematic nature of the Canaanite conquest but also by the number (and size!) of books written on the topic, start here with Trimm's short and accessible *Destruction of the Canaanites*. Trimm helpfully provides back-

ground on the ancient context, on the concept of genocide, and on the identity of Canaanites, before carefully working through possible interpretational solutions to the problem. I'm confident that readers will greatly appreciate, as I did, Trimm's wisdom and perspective on this difficult subject."

— **David T. Lamb**
Missio Seminary

"Here is an honest engagement with one of the longstanding ethical problems raised by the Bible, marked by dialogue among diverse perspectives, fair assessment of their strengths and weaknesses, and an invitation for readers to join an ongoing conversation whose conclusions have not been predetermined. The book reads like a class discussion guided by a wise teacher committed to generous, multiperspectival dialogue. Trimm's attention to the realities of ancient warfare, the historical Canaanites, and modern genocide studies adds a depth rarely seen in similar treatments, even as the book's brevity makes it a usable primer to resource a more extensive—and still all-too-needed—discussion about God, violence, and the Bible."

— **Brad E. Kelle**
Point Loma Nazarene University

THE DESTRUCTION
OF THE CANAANITES

God, Genocide, and Biblical Interpretation

∼

CHARLIE TRIMM

WILLIAM B. EERDMANS PUBLISHING COMPANY
GRAND RAPIDS, MICHIGAN

Wm. B. Eerdmans Publishing Co.
4035 Park East Court SE, Grand Rapids, Michigan 49546
www.eerdmans.com

Published 2022
Printed in the United States of America

28 27 26 25 24 23 22   1 2 3 4 5 6 7

ISBN 978-0-8028-7962-2

Library of Congress Cataloging-in-Publication Data

Names: Trimm, Charlie, 1977– author.
Title: The destruction of the Canaanites : God, genocide, & biblical interpretation / Charlie Trimm.
Description: Grand Rapids, Michigan : William B. Eerdmans Publishing Com-
  pany, 2022. | Includes bibliographical references and index. | Summary:
  "An exploration of the ethical problem of Old Testament violence, with
  relevant background information and a survey of four different approaches
  to making sense of the Israelite destruction of the Canaanites"—Provided
  by publisher.
Identifiers: LCCN 2021033068 | ISBN 9780802879622
Subjects: LCSH: Violence in the Bible. | Genocide—Biblical teaching. |
  Canaanites—Biblical teaching. | Bible. Old Testament—Criticism, interpre-
  tation, etc. | BISAC: RELIGION / Biblical Criticism & Interpretation / Old
  Testament | POLITICAL SCIENCE / Genocide & War Crimes
Classification: LCC BS1199.V56 T75 2022 | DDC 241/.697—dc23
LC record available at https://lccn.loc.gov/2021033068

Quotations of the Bible follow the English Standard Version unless
otherwise noted.

CONTENTS

ABBREVIATIONS

ABL	*Assyrian and Babylonian Letters Belonging to the Kouyunjik Collections of the British Museum.* Edited by Robert F. Harper. 14 vols. Chicago: University of Chicago Press, 1892–1914.
AEL	*Ancient Egyptian Literature.* Miriam Lichtheim. 3 vols. Berkeley: University of California Press, 1971–1980.
ANEP	Pritchard, James B., ed. *The Ancient Near East in Pictures Relating to the Old Testament.* 2nd ed. Princeton: Princeton University Press, 1994.
ANET	Pritchard, James B., ed. *Ancient Near Eastern Texts Relating to the Old Testament.* 3rd ed. Princeton: Princeton University Press, 1969.
AOAT	Alter Orient und Altes Testament
AOS	American Oriental Series
ARM	Archives Royales de Mari
BASOR	*Bulletin of the American Schools of Oriental Research*
BBRSup	Bulletin for Biblical Research Supplements
BJS	Brown Judaic Studies
BM	British Museum
BZAW	Beihefte zur Zeitschrift für die alttestamentliche Wissenschaft
CBQ	*Catholic Biblical Quarterly*
CBR	*Currents in Biblical Research*

CHANE	Culture and History of the Ancient Near East
COS	Hallo, William W., and K. Lawson Younger Jr., eds. *The Context of Scripture*. 4 vols. Leiden: Brill, 1997–2016.
EA	El-Amarna letter
ESV	English Standard Version
FAT	Forschungen zum Alten Testament
HTR	*Harvard Theological Review*
JETS	*Journal of the Evangelical Theological Society*
JJS	*Journal of Jewish Studies*
JPS	Jewish Publication Society
JSOTSup	Journal for the Study of the Old Testament Supplement Series
JTI	*Journal of Theological Interpretation*
JTISup	Journal of Theological Interpretation Supplements
NIVAC	NIV Application Commentary
OtSt	*Oudtestamentische Studiën*
RIMA 1	Grayson, A. Kirk. *Assyrian Rulers of the Third and Second Millennia BC (to 1115 BC)*. The Royal Inscriptions of Mesopotamia, Assyrian Periods 1. Toronto: University of Toronto Press, 1987.
RIMA 2	Grayson, A. Kirk. *Assyrian Rulers of the Early First Millennium BC I (1114–859 BC)*. The Royal Inscriptions of Mesopotamia, Assyrian Periods 2. Toronto: University of Toronto Press, 1991.
RIMA 3	Grayson, A. Kirk. *Assyrian Rulers of the Early First Millennium BC II (858–745 BC)*. The Royal Inscriptions of Mesopotamia, Assyrian Periods 3. Toronto: University of Toronto Press, 1996.
RINAP 1	Tadmor, Hayim, and Shigeo Yamada. *The Royal Inscriptions of Tiglath-pileser III (744–727 BC) and Shalmaneser V (726–722 BC), Kings of Assyria*. Royal Inscriptions of the Neo-Assyrian Period 1. Winona Lake, IN: Eisenbrauns, 2011.
RINAP 2	Frame, Grant. *The Royal Inscriptions of Sargon II, King*

of Assyria (721–705 BC). Royal Inscriptions of the Neo-Assyrian Period 2. University Park: Eisenbrauns, 2021.

RINAP 3/1   Grayson, A. Kirk, and Jamie Novotny. *The Royal Inscriptions of Sennacherib, King of Assyria (704–681 BC), Part 1*. Royal Inscriptions of the Neo-Assyrian Period 3/1. Winona Lake, IN: Eisenbrauns, 2012.

RINAP 3/2   Grayson, A. Kirk, and Jamie Novotny. *The Royal Inscriptions of Sennacherib, King of Assyria (704–681 BC), Part 2*. Royal Inscriptions of the Neo-Assyrian Period 3/2. Winona Lake, IN: Eisenbrauns, 2014.

RINAP 4   Leichty, Erle. *The Royal Inscriptions of Esarhaddon, King of Assyria (680–669 BC)*. Royal Inscriptions of the Neo-Assyrian Period 4. Winona Lake, IN: Eisenbrauns, 2011.

RINAP 5/1   Novotny, Jamie, and Joshua Jeffers. *The Royal Inscriptions of Ashurbanipal (668–631 BC, Assur-etal-ilani (630–627 BC), and Sin-sarra-iskun (626–612 BC), Kings of Assyria, Part 1*. Royal Inscriptions of the Neo-Assyrian Period 5/1. Winona Lake, IN: Eisenbrauns, 2018.

RITA   Kitchen, K. A. *Ramesside Inscriptions Translated and Annotated: Translations*. 7 vols. Oxford: Blackwell, 1993–2014.

SAA 1   Parpola, Simo. *The Correspondence of Sargon II, Part 1: Letters from Assyria and the West*. State Archives of Assyria 1. Helsinki: Helsinki University Press, 1987.

SAA 2   Parpola, Simo, and Kazuko Watanabe. *Neo-Assyrian Treaties and Loyalty Oaths*. State Archives of Assyria 2. Helsinki: Helsinki University Press, 1988.

SAA 16   Luukko, Mikko, and Greta Van Buylaere. *The Political Correspondence of Esarhaddon*. State Archives of Assyria 16. Helsinki: Helsinki University Press, 2002.

SAA 19   Luukko, Mikko. *The Correspondence of Tiglath-pileser III and Sargon II from Calah/Nimrud*. State Archives of Assyria 19. Helsinki: The Neo-Assyrian Text Corpus Project, 2012.

SBLWAW	Society of Biblical Literature Writings from the Ancient World
SJOT	*Scandinavian Journal of the Old Testament*
SLA	Pfeiffer, Robert H. *State Letters of Assyria: A Transliteration and Translation of 355 Official Letters Dating from the Sargonid Period (722–625 B.C.).* AOS 6. New Haven: American Oriental Society, 1935.
TynBul	*Tyndale Bulletin*
VCSup	Vigiliae Christianae Supplements
VT	*Vetus Testamentum*
VTSup	Supplements to Vetus Testamentum
WTJ	*Westminster Theological Journal*
WUNT	Wissenschaftliche Untersuchungen zum Neuen Testament
ZAW	*Zeitschrift für die alttestamentliche Wissenschaft*

INTRODUCTION

Looking back throughout history, we can see many examples of humans engaging in horrific behavior. Among all of these sordid parts of our history, however, genocide is surely among the worst. The most well-known is the killing of six million Jews in the German Holocaust during World War II, but many other lesser-known genocides have also occurred in places like Rwanda, Turkey, and Cambodia. As depressing as these accounts of genocides are, for Christians reading stories of mass slaughter in the Old Testament is even more disturbing. Some of these accounts can be rationalized by noting that YHWH disapproved of them, such as the slaughter of the people of Shechem by Jacob's sons Simeon and Levi (Gen. 34; 49:5–7).[1] However, such a neat separation between genocide instigated by humankind and that sanctioned by YHWH is difficult to maintain across the Old Testament. For example, YHWH's commands to Israel in Deuteronomy 7:1–2 sound suspiciously like genocide.

> When the LORD your God brings you into the land that you are entering to take possession of it, and clears away many nations before you, the Hittites, the Girgashites, the Amorites, the Canaanites, the Perizzites, the Hivites, and the Jebusites, seven nations more numerous and mightier than you, and when the LORD your

1. YHWH is the revealed name of God in the Old Testament and is commonly translated as LORD in modern translations.

God gives them over to you, and you defeat them, then you must devote them to complete destruction. You shall make no covenant with them and show no mercy to them.

One way to describe the problem that readers of the Old Testament face when they encounter these violent texts is through the lens of moral injury, the moral harm done to soldiers as they participate in warfare. Brad Kelle defines moral injury as "a nonphysical wound that results from the violation of a person's core moral beliefs (by oneself or others)."[2] This moral injury is particularly prevalent in situations where officers order soldiers to follow immoral commands. Kelle has helpfully applied this concept to the Old Testament: the deity that readers expect to be kind and merciful has acted in ways that are seemingly immoral and trauma-inducing for his followers.[3] He provides two observations from moral injury scholarship that are helpful for addressing this problem by engaging in moral repair. First, he emphasizes the need to "create conversations around the morally injurious experiences"[4] and second, he states that moral repair requires "the need to communalize morally wounding experiences so that a sense of shared responsibility emerges for both the injurious circumstances and the work of healing and restoration."[5]

My goal in this book is not to tell you the "correct answer" to the ethical problem of the destruction of the Canaanites. Instead, I want to help you see a fuller picture of the problem and walk with you through various proposed solutions, highlighting their strengths and weaknesses. At heart, following Kelle's suggestions, I desire to introduce you to the conversation as part of the process of moral repair. My hope is that this book will serve as a springboard for communities to gather in order to continue this important conversation.

2. Brad E. Kelle, *The Bible and Moral Injury: Reading Scripture Alongside War's Unseen Wounds* (Nashville: Abingdon, 2020), 2.

3. Kelle, *Bible and Moral Injury*, 139–68.

4. Kelle, *Bible and Moral Injury*, 163.

5. Kelle, *Bible and Moral Injury*, 164. Kelle also has a third path to moral repair—lament—which will be discussed at the end of this book.

We will begin our journey with some background to help us understand the problem of the destruction of the Canaanites in its historical context. A survey of warfare in the ancient Near East, which, for the purposes of this book, will roughly include the time frame of about 2000 to 500 BCE and the territory from Egypt in the south to Mesopotamia in the east, will help us learn how battles were normally conducted (chapter one).[6] Following this survey we will learn the history and definition of genocide (chapter two), and the identity of the Canaanites (chapter three).

The second part of the book will address four categories of responses to the Canaanite problem: reevaluating God (chapter four), the Old Testament (chapter five), the interpretation of the Old Testament (chapter six), and violence in the Old Testament (chapter seven).

6. The material in this section is a brief summary of Charlie Trimm, *Fighting for the King and the Gods: A Survey of Warfare in the Ancient Near East*, Resources for Biblical Literature 88 (Atlanta: Society of Biblical Literature, 2017).

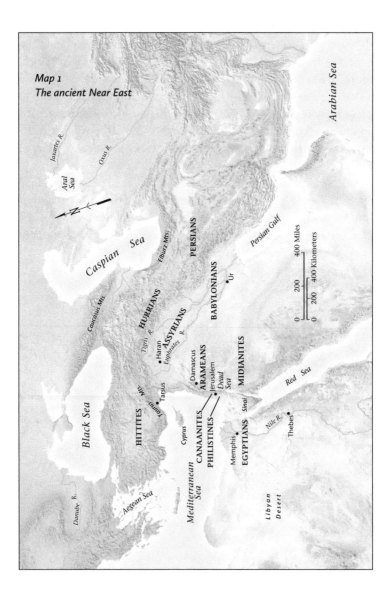

Map 1
The ancient Near East

PART ONE

Background

~

Chapter One

WARFARE IN THE ANCIENT NEAR EAST

Causes of War

Countries in the ancient Near East went to war for a variety of reasons. As might be expected, self-defense or defending an ally who was attacked were common reasons for going to war. For example, Ramses III, the pharaoh of Egypt during the twelfth century BCE, defeated the Sea People (who included the Philistines known from the Bible) when they attacked Egypt.[1] The Amarna letters, which were written mostly by Canaanite kings to Pharaoh Akhenaten around 1350 BCE, often requested help for self-defense, such as in this letter: "Moreover, note that it is the ruler of Ḥaṣura who has taken 3 cities from me. From the time I heard and verified this, there has been waging of war against him. Truly, may the king, my lord, take cognizance, and may the king, my lord, give thought to his servant."[2]

Another major reason for going to war sounds strange to modern ears: protection against chaos. Nations saw chaos as manifested in such things as broken treaties and evil deeds. Even chaos found outside their borders could be perceived as perilous because it might endanger order everywhere in the world. In modern terms, this might

---

1. "The 'Sea Peoples' Records of Ramesses III," trans. K. A. Kitchen (*COS* 4.2:11–14).

2. EA 364; translation from William L. Moran, ed. and trans., *The Amarna Letters* (Baltimore: Johns Hopkins University Press, 1992), 362.

be compared to how we approach human rights: a country might go to war to protect a minority population being oppressed within another country in order to uphold ideals of universal human rights. In Egypt, the idea of order was expressed through the term *maat*, while *isft* was the chaos that always threatened to overwhelm the world. One of the primary duties of the pharaoh was to encourage *maat* in the world and defeat *isft*.[3] Conquering a foreign country defeated the chaos there and brought order; for example, Ramses II (thirteenth century BCE) claimed that travelers were safe in the lands under Egyptian control: "Thereafter, if a man or woman went out on business to Syria, they could even reach the Hatti-land without fear haunting their minds, because of (the magnitude of) the victories of His Majesty."[4] Assyrians viewed the world in a similar way, as demonstrated by this quotation from Esarhaddon, king of the Neo-Assyrian empire in the seventh century BCE: "When the god Aššur, the great lord, (wanted) to reveal the glorious might of my deeds to the people, he . . . empowered me to loot (and) plunder (any) land (that) had committed sin, crime, (or) negligence against the god Aššur."[5]

Like today, the ancients did not describe the cause of their wars as the desire to acquire plunder, but it clearly played an important role in their decisions. For example, one king wrote to his ally about why they should go to war together: "'Fatten' your troops with spoils (so that) they will bless you."[6] In some graffiti about a military campaign, an Egyptian soldier wrote: "There was no fighting; I shall not bring a Nubian back (as captive) from the land of the Nubians."[7]

3. John Baines, "Ancient Egyptian Kingship: Official Forms, Rhetoric, Context," in *King and Messiah in Israel and the Ancient Near East: Proceedings of the Oxford Old Testament Seminar*, ed. John Day, JSOTSup 270 (Sheffield: Sheffield Academic, 1998), 41–46.

4. *RITA* 2.Ramesses II 67:99.

5. RINAP 4, 185.

6. ARM 5.16 in Jack M. Sasson, *The Military Establishment at Mari*, Studia Pohl 3 (Rome: Pontifical Biblical Institute, 1969), 48.

7. R. B. Parkinson, *Voices from Ancient Egypt: An Anthology of Middle Kingdom Writings*, Oklahoma Series in Classical Culture 9 (Norman: University of Oklahoma Press, 1991), 95.

Preparation for War

While the battles themselves attract the most attention, wise generals know that preparation for war is just as important as actually fighting the battles. Even though they did not have the sophisticated technology available to modern armies, leaders were still able to gather significant amounts of information about their enemies. In some cases foreign nationals themselves provided information to kings; indeed, an important part of being a good vassal king was keeping one's suzerain—the conquering king—informed. One Assyrian treaty with a vassal includes this clause: "[Nor] will you conceal from me anything that you hear, be it from the mouth of a king, or on account of a country, (anything) that bears upon or is harmful to us or Assyria, but you will write to me and bring it to my attention."[8] Scouting while on campaign was also important as a way to learn about local terrain, specifics about the composition of the enemy army, and the location of the enemy. Ramses II recounts a significant scouting failure when captured Hittite scouts convinced the Egyptians that the Hittite king was still at home, when in reality he was already marching to battle.[9]

Leaders also had to muster troops for the battles. Nations usually employed their own people to serve in their armies and created various means of ordering that process. However, many nations also used foreign troops in their armies. For example, after the defeat of Samaria at the hands of the Assyrians in 722 BCE, a group of Israelite charioteers served in the Assyrian army under Sargon II: "I conscripted two hundred chariots from among them into [my] royal (military) contingent."[10] In addition, an Egyptian scribal satire about the soldier's life refers to prisoners being branded when they became attendants of the army.[11]

8. SAA 2.13.
9. "The Battle of Qadesh—The 'Bulletin' Text," trans. K. A. Kitchen (*COS* 2.5B:39).
10. RINAP 2, 330.
11. Ricardo A. Caminos, *Late-Egyptian Miscellanies*, Brown Egyptological Studies 1 (London: Oxford University Press, 1954), 230.

Other major preparations for war involved either marching to the battlefield or strengthening fortifications. For long-distance marches, kings usually began their campaigns in the spring (2 Sam. 11:1). For example, Pharaoh Thutmose III began his march against Megiddo in early April, when the wheat harvest was finishing.[12] The average speed of ancient armies seems to have been around 10–13 miles per day, as they traveled on foot.[13] Nature frequently posed a danger as great as enemy soldiers. Kings often boasted of conquering mountains, deserts, or rivers in terms similar to defeating the enemy, as in this quotation from the Assyrian king Tiglath-pileser I: "In Mount Aruma, a difficult area which was impassible for my chariots, I abandoned my chariotry. Taking the lead of my warriors I slithered victoriously with the viciousness of a viper over the perilous mountain ledges."[14] Supplying water and food for these long marches was often complicated as well, since armies could only carry a limited supply with them. Armies established supply depots along campaign routes, enlisted allies to provide supplies, or forced local residents to give them provisions. While the attacking army was marching, the defenders strengthened fortifications, generally focusing on fortifying their major cities but often including outlying fortresses as well. Second Chronicles 32:1–5 provides the account of Hezekiah's fortification of Jerusalem in preparation for the arrival of the marching Assyrian army.

Battles and Weapons of War

Armies in the ancient Near East fought two main kinds of battles. First, some battles were fought in the open field, though unfortunately specific tactics for these battles are unknown. Chariots were developed in the mid-second millennium and played an important role as mobile missile platforms, allowing archers on the chariots to draw near to the enemy, fire at them, and then retreat without easily being attacked.

12. "The Annals of Thutmose III," trans. James K. Hoffmeier (*COS* 2.2A:8).
13. Trimm, *Fighting for the King and the Gods*, 129–33.
14. RIMA 2, 16.

Figure 1. Cast of Ramses II relief from Beit el-Wali. British Museum, London.

Figure 2. Cavalry of Ashurnasirpal II. British Museum, London.

Figure 3. Spearmen from the tomb of Mesehti. Cairo Museum, Egypt. Photo by Udimu / CC-BY-SA-3.0.

The supremacy of the chariot continued until cavalry took over their role around 800 BCE. The bow was the most important distance weapon in the ancient Near East: the presence of a bowman on a chariot or the back of a horse would have terrified the enemy. The most common hand-to-hand offensive weapon was the spear. Although in earlier times maces and axes were used, they were displaced by the sword. However, none of these weapons were as widespread as the spear. Defensive items such as leather or linen scale armor became more common throughout the time period, and helmets and shields were frequently used. Metal armor remained rare.

The second common kind of battle was a siege, which would have been the default choice for defenders since the large walls of major cities would have prevented a quick victory for attacking armies. During times of siege, surrounding villages were often emptied as the rural population fled to the cities. Since keeping an army in the field for a long period of time was difficult, defenders could effectively be victorious if they caused the attacker to return home. Attackers could win by remaining until the city's food supplies dwindled, causing horrific starvation conditions inside the city (2 Kings 6:25–29). Direct assaults on the city could involve the use of battering rams, tunneling, sapping, ladders, and siege towers. Defenders developed a variety of strategies against these direct assaults, such as setting siege towers on fire and building a counter ramp inside the city. One of the most famous sieges is that of the Judean city of Lachish in 701 BCE by the Assyrians.

Other kinds of battle were less common. Since the armies of the ancient Near East were largely land based, naval battles were infrequent. Also, in spite of the story of David and Goliath, single combat—in which two representatives fought each other—was very rare in the ancient Near East. Finally, deception in battle (such as the use of surprise or night attacks) was practiced at times, especially during sieges or by smaller kingdoms that had fewer choices.

Figure 4. Assyrian soldiers. Museum of the Ancient Near East, Berlin. Photo by Wolfgang Sauber / CC-BY-SA-3.0.

Figure 5. Egyptian siege by Ramses II. Ramesseum, Theban necropolis, near Luxor, Egypt.

Figure 6. Assyrian siege by Sennacherib at La-chish. British Museum, London.

Results of War

One obvious result of battle for the defeated was flight, which the victors loved to describe with vivid metaphors. For example, Sennacherib, king of the Neo-Assyrian Empire in the seventh century BCE, said, "They abandoned their tents and, in order to save their lives, they trampled the corpses of their troops as they pushed on. Their hearts throbbed like the pursued young of pigeons, they passed their urine hotly, (and) released their excrement inside their chariots."[15] The immediate action of the victors was often to take plunder: Thutmose III rebuked his troops for plundering the enemy before the battle was even over.[16] Plunder and prisoners were primarily given to the king and the gods, though individual soldiers also received a share. In some cases rewards were given to soldiers based on how many enemies they killed as proven by severed hands.

Victorious kings sometimes destroyed the cities, crops, and trees of their enemies. They also often humiliated the defeated enemies in

---

15. RINAP 3/1, 184.
16. "The Annals of Thutmose III," trans. James K. Hoffmeier (COS 2.2A:11).

Figure 7. Counting hands in a relief by Ramses III. Medinet Habu, Egypt.
Photo by Asta.

a variety of ways, focusing their attention on enemy leaders. In Egypt, for example, the top of the sole of Tutankhamun's sandals depicted prisoners, enabling him to constantly "walk" on his enemies. Pharaoh Amenhotep II exhibited the dead bodies of his enemies: "His majesty returned in joy of heart to his father Amon, when he had slain with his own mace the seven princes who had been in the district of Takhshi, who had been put upside down at the prow of his majesty's falcon-boat."[17] One officer recommended to a king in Mesopotamia during the eighteenth century that he take brutal measures to spread news of his victory: "Let them escort their two surviving (Yaminite) *ḫana* to the border, and then at the border, mutilate them. Let their survivors go to the Yaminites in order to proclaim that my lord has captured the town of Mišlan by force."[18] The Assyrians often impaled

17. *ANET*, 248.
18. ARM 26.282 in Daniel E. Fleming, *Democracy's Ancient Ancestors: Mari and Early Collective Governance* (Cambridge: Cambridge University Press, 2004), 92.

Figure 8. *(above)* Assyrians crushing the bones of rebels. British Museum, London. Drawing from Layard, *A Second Series of the Monuments of Nineveh* (London: J. Murray, 1853), plate 47.

Figure 9. *(right)* Sandals of Tutankhamun. Cairo Museum, Egypt.

enemy leaders. Ashurbanipal forced one set of rebels to crush the bones of their father, which might be illustrated in one of his reliefs.[19] The purpose behind this torture was to warn other nations not to rebel, otherwise this would be their fate as well. However, extermination of the enemy was rare, as will be discussed in chapter 2.

The political results of conquest varied. Sometimes attacks were merely raids for the sake of plunder or vengeance that had no lasting political implications. However, stronger kingdoms sometimes exercised greater influence over their conquered territory. The first step was forcing the conquered king to enter into a suzerain-vassal relationship, in which the suzerain (the conquering king) promised to protect the vassal (the conquered king) and the vassal promised to provide tribute. If the vassal rebelled, then the next step was to replace him with another king who would be more amenable to the suzerain's

19. RINAP 5/1, 73; Austen H. Layard, *A Second Series of the Monuments of Nineveh Including Bas-Reliefs from the Palace of Sennacherib and Bronzes from the Ruins of Nimroud from Drawings Made on the Spot During a Second Expedition to Assyria* (London: J. Murray, 1853), plate 45.

demands. If an area repeatedly rebelled, it could be placed directly under the supervision of the suzerain as a province of the empire.

Gods and Warfare

Everything was infused with the divine in the ancient Near East. The gods were frequently depicted as fighting chaos in myths like Enuma Elish (a Mesopotamian creation myth) and the Ugaritic Baal Cycle, and were portrayed as divine warriors in reliefs. When kings were attacked, they often called on the gods for help and performed rituals

Figure 10. Assyrian impaling of prisoners by Sennacherib at Lachish. British Museum, London.

before battle to ensure the gods' participation. One Egyptian ritual involved writing the names of protective deities on balls and throwing them against each of the four cardinal points (each representing an area ruled by Egypt: Nubia, Asia, Libya, and Upper and Lower Egypt).[20]

Ramses II prayed during a battle: "Indeed, what's up with you, my father Amun? Has a father ever ignored his son? Now, have I

20. Lana Troy, "Religion and Cult during the Time of Thutmose III," in *Thutmose III: A New Biography*, ed. Eric H. Cline and David O'Connor (Ann Arbor: University of Michigan Press, 2006), 151–52.

done anything without you? . . . What are they to you, O Amun, these Asiatics, despicable and ignorant of God! Have I not made

for you monuments in great multitude? I have filled your temple with my captures!" Amun responded, "Forward, I am with you, I am your father, my hand is with you! I am more useful to you than hundred-thousands of men, I am the Lord of Victory, who loves bravery."[21] The Assyrian kings acted the same way. A ritual could be done on a chariot to protect a prince or a king on campaign if the chariot broke.[22] Before one battle, Sennacherib recorded that "I myself prayed to the deities Aššur, Sîn, Šamaš, Bēl, Nergal, Ištar of Nineveh, (and) Ištar of Arbela, the gods who support me, for victory over (my) strong enemy and they immediately heeded my prayer (and) came to my aid."[23]

Figure 11. The god Adad on a bull from Arslan Tash. Louvre, Paris.

The kings also spoke of the gods as being present with them in battle, and, in rare cases, even causing nature miracles to help them. Pharaoh Merneptah referred to "every god being his magical protection."[24] Thutmose III described a shooting star affecting the battle against some Asiatic enemies: "a star approached, coming to the south of them. The like had not happened before. It shot straight toward them (the enemy), not one of them could stand [. . .] falling headlong."[25] The god Ashur appears in

21. "The Battle of Qadesh—the Poem, or Literary Record," trans. K. A. Kitchen (*COS* 2.5A:34–35).

22. Stefan M. Maul, *Zukunftsbewältigung: Eine Untersuchung altorientalischen Denkens anhand der babylonisch-assyrischen Löserituale (Namburbi)*, Baghdader Forschungen 18 (Mainz: von Zabern, 1994), 397.

23. RINAP 3/1, 182.

24. *RITA* 4.Merneptah 2:2.

25. "The Gebel Barkal Stela of Thutmose III," trans. James K. Hoffmeier (*COS* 2.2B:17).

Figure 12. Ashur shooting the enemy with Ashurnasirpal II. British Museum, London.

reliefs helping the Assyrian king, often in the same pose as the king.[26] According to Tiglath-pileser III, "fear of the brilliance of (the god) Aššur, my lord, overwhelmed him and he came to the city Sapīya (Šapīya), before me, and kissed my feet."[27] Esarhaddon recounted how the god Marduk rescued him in a siege: "In the dead of night, they sprinkled with naphtha the ramp that I constructed against Uppume, his royal city, and set fire (to it). By the command of the god Marduk, king of the gods, the north wind, the sweet breeze of the lord of the gods, blew and turned the tongue(s) of roaring flame back on the city Uppume. (The fire) did not se[ize] the ramp [. . .] it burned its wall and turned (it) into ashes."[28]

Rhetoric of Warfare

It will not be surprising to learn that the texts and reliefs of ancient Near Eastern kings did not always reflect reality because they were composed to glorify the king. However, while it is often difficult to verify, it appears that the kings did not create accomplishments for themselves out of thin air. Instead, their self-aggrandizing rhetoric

26. *ANEP*, 180, no. 536 (BM 115706).
27. RINAP 1, 120.
28. RINAP 4, 82–83.

mainly focused on which events to talk about and how to describe those events. At a basic level, the kings almost universally ignore their own defeats. One of the very few examples is from the Assyrian king Sennacherib, who admitted that his army was defeated by Babylon; however, he felt safe to record this because he was not personally present on the battlefield and responded quickly to address the defeat.[29] While armies employed complicated command structures of officers to facilitate leading armies and kings would have been highly dependent upon officers to achieve victory, kings largely ignored the contributions of officers in their annals except in cases like this when defeat could be blamed on them. Letters are marginally more forthcoming about defeats, such as a report to Tiglath-pileser III about a defeat at the hands of Urartu.[30]

Kings also tended to employ hyperbole about their victories, and texts frequently praise the prowess of the king in battle. For example, the Assyrian king Sargon II professed that "with (only) my personal chariot and the horse(men) that go at my side . . . , I fell upon him (Rusâ) like a fierce arrow, inflicted a defeat on him, and turned back his attack."[31] Another Assyrian king named Tukulti-Ninurta I claimed that "in the midst of that battle I captured Kaštiliašu, king of the Kassites, (and) trod with my feet upon his lordly neck as though it were a footstool."[32] Ramses II of Egypt said he attacked the enemy by himself:

> Then His Majesty set forth at a gallop, he plunged into the midst of the forces of the Hittite foe, he being entirely on his own, no-one else with him. So, His Majesty went on to look around him; he found 2,500 chariot-spans hemming him in, all around him, even all the champions ("runners") of the Hittite foe, along with

29. RINAP 3/1, 33.
30. SAA 19.71.
31. RINAP 2, 287.
32. RIMA 1, 245.

the numerous foreign countries who were with them. . . . But there was no high officer with me, no charioteer, no army-soldier, no shield-bearer.[33]

Given the lack of comparative data, the degree of hyperbole in such statements is difficult to determine. However, it can be seen indirectly in a few areas. First, archaeology and history demonstrate that kings did at times engage directly in battle. The mummy of Seqenenre-Tao of the 17th Dynasty appears to have been killed in battle by an axe,[34] and the Assyrian king Sargon II died in battle.[35] However, other texts (especially letters) paint a different picture of their role in battle. Ramses II himself admitted that his portrayal of being alone in battles was hyperbolic when he described his conversation with his shield-bearer in the middle of the battle described above.[36] Likewise, even though Ramses III claimed he fought the Sea People by himself—"Power amid a multitude and unequalled, he strikes down millions, alone, by himself"[37]—in his reliefs he depicted his army at his side fighting the enemy.[38] While the Egyptian princes were expected to be powerful warriors like their fathers, a relief of the Battle of Qadesh includes a command to keep the princes out of battle: "The arrival of the Fan-bearer of Pharaoh, LPH, to tell the Royal Children . . . '[Do not ?] leave by the West side of the camp, keep yourselves clear of the battle!'"[39] A letter to Esarhaddon of Assyria

33. "The Battle of Qadesh—The Poem, or Literary Record," trans. K. A. Kitchen (*COS* 2.5A:34).

34. Joyce M. Filer, "Ancient Egypt and Nubia as a Source of Information for Cranial Injuries," in *Material Harm: Archaeological Studies of War and Violence*, ed. John Carman (Glasgow: Cruithne, 1997), 65–66.

35. J.-J. Glassner, *Mesopotamian Chronicles*, ed. Benjamin R. Foster, SBLWAW 19 (Atlanta: Society of Biblical Literature, 2004), 174–75.

36. "The Battle of Qadesh—The Poem, or Literary Record," trans. K. A. Kitchen (*COS* 2.5A:36).

37. *RITA* 5.Ramses III 9:32–33.

38. *ANEP*, 114, no. 341.

39. *RITA* 2.Ramsses II 3C:19.

instructed him to avoid personal battle: "The king, my lord, should not advance [to the b]attle. [Just a]s your royal fathers have done, st[ay] on the hill, and [let] your [ma]gnates [do] the bat[tle]."[40]

Second, the number of friendly casualties is usually vastly underestimated. Pepi-Nakht (during the Egyptian sixth dynasty) wrote that Pepi II sent him to gather the bodies of several slain Egyptians, one of the very few references to friendly casualties in Egyptian literature.[41] Sargon II noted several Assyrian casualties in a "letter to the god": "one charioteer, two cavalrymen, (and) three *light infantrymen* were killed."[42] These are most likely not literal numbers, but a standardized rhetorical phrase since it also appears in other examples of the genre.[43] Letters provide the clearest evidence for friendly casualties, including references to widows of fallen soldiers[44] and the request of a son whose father had died in enemy lands.[45] Another letter reports that a group of 150 Assyrian soldiers had been victorious in battle, but twenty Assyrians were wounded. However, these examples are exceptional: the vast majority of literature about battles completely ignores casualties.[46]

Third, the extent of the victory is often overestimated. This is seen most clearly in cases when records remain of both sides claiming victory in a battle, such as the battle between the Hittites and the Egyptians at Qadesh. Later letters between the two sides sent after the signing of a peace treaty continued the debate.[47] Another example is Sennacherib's victory at Halule over a Babylonian and Elamite coalition in which he claimed that he filled the battlefield with corpses, killed many enemy leaders, and forced the kings of Elam and Bab-

40. SAA 16.77.
41. *AEL* 1:163.
42. RINAP 2, 306–7. Italics in original.
43. RINAP 4, 85 and RIMA 3, 244.
44. SAA 1.21.
45. SAA 16.105.
46. *ABL* 520/*SLA* 43.
47. Trevor Bryce, *Letters of the Great Kings of the Ancient Near East: The Royal Correspondence of the Late Bronze Age* (London: Routledge, 2003), 89–90.

ylon to flee.[48] However, the Babylonian Chronicle records that the Assyrians withdrew.[49] While the Assyrians might have won a tactical victory, the Babylonians achieved a strategic victory by keeping their army largely intact and forcing the Assyrians into a long siege of Babylon.[50]

Even in battles where texts from the other side are not known, it is clear that kings sometimes overestimated their victory. Rather famously, the first reference to Israel outside the Bible comes in a statement of its total destruction by Merneptah: "Israel is wasted, its seed is not."[51] Likewise, Thutmose III claimed that he completely destroyed an enemy army: "Numerous armies of Mitanni were overthrown in the space of an hour, annihilated completely like those who had not existed, in the manner of those who are burned."[52] Not only is the phrase "in the space of an hour" hyperbolic, but Mitanni does not seem to have been substantially weakened and Thutmose III was not able to hold any territory of Mitanni.[53]

Sennacherib was infuriated by the continual rebellion of Babylon against Assyrian rule: "I removed the brick(s) and earth, as much as there was, from the (inner) wall and outer wall, the temples, (and) the ziggurat, (and) I threw (it) into the Araḫtu river. . . . So that in the future, the site of that city and (its) temples will be unrecognizable, I dissolved it (Babylon) in water and annihilated (it), (making it)

48. RINAP 3/1, 182–84.

49. Glassner, *Mesopotamian Chronicles*, 198–99.

50. Sarah C. Melville, "Win, Lose, or Draw? Claiming Victory in Battle," in *Krieg und Frieden im Alten Vorderasien: 52e Rencontre Assyriologique Internationale International Congress of Assyriology and Near Eastern Archaeology Münster, 17.-21. Juli 2006*, ed. Hans Neumann et al., AOAT 401 (Münster: Ugarit-Verlag, 2014), 533–34.

51. "The (Israel) Stela of Merneptah," trans. James K. Hoffmeier (*COS* 2.6:41).

52. "The Gebel Barkal Stela of Thutmose III," trans. James K. Hoffmeier (*COS* 2.2B:15).

53. On the history of Mitanni, see Amélie Kuhrt, *The Ancient Near East c. 3000–330 BC*, 2 vols., Routledge History of the Ancient World (London: Routledge, 1995), 1:289–96.

like a meadow."[54] However, while Babylon surely suffered, it was not stamped out of existence and was recognized by Esarhaddon, the son of Sennacherib.[55]

In sum, it appears that while ancient Near Eastern kings did not invent stories of war, they clearly recounted events with rhetorical flourishes that downplayed the negative aspects of the account, emphasized the aspects that glorified them and their gods, and employed hyperbole with respect to the extent of their victories.[56]

---

54. RINAP 3/2, 316–17.

55. For details on this history, see Kuhrt, *Ancient Near East*, 2:582–87.

56. For more on different kinds of hyperbole in the ancient Near East, including numerical, speed, severity, extent, and attribution, see William J. Webb and Gordon K. Oeste, *Bloody, Brutal, and Barbaric: Wrestling with Troubling War Texts* (Downers Grove, IL: IVP Academic, 2019), 136–50.

Chapter Two

GENOCIDE

Genocide throughout History

The most famous genocide in the minds of most today is the German Holocaust, in which Adolf Hitler and his Nazi party oppressed the German Jews in a variety of ways and eventually murdered six million Jews across Europe. While anti-Semitism is the aspect of the Nazi repression most commonly remembered, they also killed many other groups of people, including homosexuals, Russian prisoners of war, the Romani, and various individuals with disabilities.

However, the Holocaust is far from the only genocide. Genocides can be divided into two broad categories.[1] First, a colonial genocide is one in which an aggressor travels elsewhere to destroy another group, often to take possession of their land. Examples include the Spanish conquest of the New World, the Japanese invasion of Korea in 1567–1598, the English conquest of Ireland in 1565–1603, and the British colonization of North America and Australia. A particularly important colonial genocide was the German massacre of the Herero people in southwestern Africa in 1904, as it provided precedent for German practices during the Holocaust.[2] In the colonization of North America, disease was the primary agent of death among the

---

1. Ben Kiernan, *Blood and Soil: A World History of Genocide and Extermination from Sparta to Darfur* (New Haven: Yale University Press, 2009).
2. Kiernan, *Blood and Soil*, 374–90.

Native Americans—and this was not entirely accidental, as sometimes disease was intentionally spread among them by Europeans. Other deaths were caused by the destruction of their living areas and expulsion from their traditional homes, most famously in the Trail of Tears in which the United States government forcibly moved the Cherokees and other groups out of the southeastern United States, causing around a third of them to die on the journey. Finally, genocidal massacres of Native Americans were not uncommon; the Sand Creek massacre of 1864 stands out as a particularly brutal example, in which several hundred Cheyenne and Arapaho—mostly women and children—were killed and mutilated.[3]

The second category of genocide is an internal genocide. The pattern for this category of genocide is that a more powerful group decimates a less powerful group in their own midst. A famous example is the Turkish genocide of around a million Armenians and other Christians—Assyrians and Greeks—during World War I.[4] This genocide was encouraged by the desperation associated with the decline of the Ottoman Empire and the vulnerability of the Christians in the remaining parts of the empire. Massacres of Armenians were committed in 1894–1896, but the majority of the deaths occurred during the First World War when official government documents spelled out the enforced removal of Armenians to the east to "wipe them out either on the road or there."[5] In addition, the plan called for the army to "exterminate" all teachers, priests, and males under the age of fifty and to forcibly convert girls and children to Islam.[6] On their journey east many were taken or killed by local populations, and violent prisoners were even released to expand the killing. The United States ambassador to Turkey, Henry Morgenthau Sr., describes how one group of Armenians began with 18,000 people and arrived at their

3. Kiernan, *Blood and Soil*, 213–48, 310–63; Adam Jones, *Genocide: A Comprehensive Introduction*, 3rd ed. (New York: Routledge, 2017), 153–63.

4. For a survey of the Armenian Genocide, see Kiernan, *Blood and Soil*, 395–415.

5. Kiernan, *Blood and Soil*, 408.

6. Kiernan, *Blood and Soil*, 408.

destination in the east with a mere 150 people. The Turks justified the genocide by calling it a military operation against rebels, removing a population that was sympathetic to their enemies. Turkey to this day denies that the massacres happened. Hitler famously said in the context of his command to kill the Polish people (including women and children), "*Who, after all, talks nowadays of the annihilation of the Armenians?*"[7]

Another famous example of an internal genocide is the slaughter of the Tutsis by the Hutus in Rwanda in 1994, in which one million people died.[8] When the colonial Europeans initially arrived in the area, the Hutus and Tutsis were not really two different people groups, but were more like different castes: the richer Tutsis owned cattle while the Hutus were farmers and tended to be poorer. Europeans solidified the boundaries between these two groups as part of the common colonial technique of dividing and conquering local inhabitants. A genealogy was even created to differentiate the two groups: the Hutus, descended from Ham, were destined to be slaves (see chapter three on the curse of Ham), while the Tutsis, descended from the ancient Egyptians, were by nature leaders. The number of the dead in the genocide was significantly less than the six million Jews killed in the Holocaust, but the rate of death was much higher because it lasted only one hundred days. In addition, the killing was largely committed by civilians with hand-to-hand weapons and happened even in supposedly safe places like churches. The Rwandan genocide remains one of the clearest examples of a time when the international community should have acted more forcefully and quickly to protect a threatened population.

Unfortunately, this kind of genocide continues unabated today. Groups like Genocide Watch provide up-to-date information about places worldwide where genocide might be happening.[9] However, since countries are rarely honest about genocides occurring in their

---

7. Jones, *Genocide*, 200. Italics in original.

8. Jones, *Genocide*, 473–87; Kiernan, *Blood and Soil*, 554–68.

9. www.genocidewatch.com.

midst, the identity and extent of genocides frequently become apparent only in retrospect, hindering efforts to prevent them.

Definition of Genocide

While the definition of genocide might seem intuitive, it is surprisingly contested. The word was originally coined by a Jewish lawyer named Raphaël Lemkin in the 1940s.[10] After rejecting a few other words, he created the word "genocide" by combining the Greek word *genos* ("people") with the suffix *-cide*, from the Latin word *caedo* ("cut, kill"). Lemkin began his research with the killings of the Armenians, but knowledge about the Holocaust began to circulate as his work progressed. The high point of Lemkin's work was the UN Convention on the Prevention and Punishment of the Crime of Genocide in 1948:

> In the present Convention, genocide means any of the following acts committed with intent to destroy, in whole or in part, a national, ethnical, racial or religious group, as such:
> (a) Killing members of the group;
> (b) Causing serious bodily or mental harm to members of the group;
> (c) Deliberately inflicting on the group conditions of life calculated to bring about its physical destruction in whole or in part;
> (d) Imposing measures intended to prevent births within the group;
> (e) Forcibly transferring children of the group to another group.[11]

10. Raphaël Lemkin, *Axis Rule in Occupied Europe: Laws of Occupation, Analysis of Government, and Proposals for Redress* (Washington, DC: Carnegie Endowment for International Peace, 1944).

11. For the full text, see http://www.preventgenocide.org/law/convention/text .htm.

While scholars of genocide studies today recognize the importance of this definition, most disagree with it to some extent. The standard textbook for genocide studies, Adam Jones's *Genocide: A Comprehensive Introduction*, lists twenty-five different definitions.[12] Even the core part of the definition, that genocide consists of killing because of some kind of group identity, has been disputed by Israel Charny, who has completely removed the group criterion from the definition by defining genocide in this way: "The mass killing of substantial numbers of human beings, when not in the course of military action against the military forces of an avowed enemy, under conditions of the essential defenselessness and helplessness of the victims."[13] However, most genocide scholars agree that the group criterion is an important part of defining genocide.

In spite of this agreement about the group criterion, scholars dispute which groups should be included in the definition. In Lemkin's original formulation of the definition in *Axis Rule in Occupied Europe*, political parties were included among the group identifications. However, this particular group identification was dropped from the UN Convention definition, partly because it was felt that participation in political parties was less permanent than the other groups. It has frequently been suggested that the Soviets were actively opposed to its inclusion because of the danger of prosecution based on Stalin's killing of many peasants, but it seems that Lemkin himself might have removed this criterion as part of his quest to get the Convention passed.[14] Many genocide scholars today would advocate for the inclusion of political parties into the definition of genocide.

12. Jones, *Genocide*, 23–27. For a discussion of the problem of defining genocide, see David Moshman, "Conceptions of Genocide and Perceptions of History," in *The Historiography of Genocide*, ed. Dan Stone (Hampshire: Palgrave Macmillan, 2008), 71–92.

13. Israel Charny, "Toward a Generic Definition of Genocide," in *Genocide: Conceptual and Historical Dimensions*, ed. George J. Andreopoulos (Philadelphia: University of Pennsylvania Press, 1994), 75.

14. Anton Weiss-Wendt, "When the End Justifies the Means: Raphaël Lemkin and the Shaping of a Popular Discourse on Genocide," *Genocide Studies and Prevention: An International Journal* 13.1 (2019): 173–88.

The many proposed definitions can be roughly placed on a spectrum of tighter and looser conceptions of genocide and partially correlate with the purpose of the definition.[15] The more restrictive definitions focus on mass killing and are commonly used in legal contexts for the purpose of convicting someone of genocide. Looser restrictions are generally used by scholars who want to compare and contrast various events. For them, including more events than mass killing helps to create a larger database for more secure scholarly observations and greater insight into how to prevent future genocides. One example of the contrast between the two ends of the spectrum is the debate over whether the destruction of cultural items—bombing of libraries, for example—should be called "cultural genocide." The more restrictive definitions tend to exclude such events from discussions of genocide, while the broader definitions would include them.

Ethnic cleansing is similar to genocide, but does not have an internationally accepted definition like genocide. It is usually associated with geography and the removal of a people group from a particular area. However, ethnic cleansing correlates with genocide when these forced removals lead to large numbers of people dying and the destruction of a group identity (like in the Armenian genocide).[16] This distinction between genocide and ethnic cleansing will be important for some of the arguments about the Canaanites in chapter six.

Genocide in the Ancient Near East

With this background we can now address the question of whether genocide happened in the ancient Near East. One simple way to respond to this question is to follow the stream of scholars who argue that genocide is a distinctly modern phenomenon, which would log-

15. Jones, *Genocide*, 28–34.

16. Benjamin Lieberman, "'Ethnic Cleansing' versus Genocide?" in *The Oxford Handbook of Genocide Studies*, ed. Donald Bloxham and A. Dirk Moses (Oxford: Oxford University Press, 2010), 42–60.

ically mean that ancient events cannot be described as genocide.[17] However, for the sake of discussion, we will look at events in the ancient Near East to see if they conform to the definition included in the UN Convention on Genocide.[18] As noted earlier, war atrocities were certainly a part of ancient Near Eastern warfare, which has led some scholars to label the events as genocidal.[19] However, extermination of the enemy and the killing of civilians was surprisingly uncommon: this was not standard warfare practice. Besides the Old Testament, the clearest of the few cases known include the killing of the Ya'ilanum tribe recorded in the Mari letters, the Hittite consecration of conquered cities to the storm god, the Moabite killing of Israelites recorded in the Mesha Stela, the Assyrian king Ashurnasirpal's killing of the people of Tela, and the Assyrian destruction of the city of Babylon under Sennacherib.[20]

The Hittite consecration of captured cities, in which no people were actually killed, would fit only under a broader definition that included the concept of cultural genocide. However, other events—those connected to Mesha, the Ya'ilanum tribe, Ashurnasirpal, and Sennacherib—could be considered genocide according to the standard definition. In spite of this apparent overlap, their identification as genocide remains questionable because, as exemplified by the Assyrian empire, groups in ancient times were viewed differently. The Assyrians certainly killed people from other groups, but they did not appear to kill them *because* they were part of that group. For example, Assyrian kings often spoke of making conquered peoples into Assyrians. Tiglath-pileser III deported the inhabitants of Bit-Sangibuti and

17. For examples of this view, see Zygmunt Bauman, *Modernity and the Holocaust* (Ithaca, NY: Cornell University Press, 2000); Mark Levene, *Genocide in the Age of the Nation-State 1: The Meaning of Genocide* (London: Tauris, 2005).

18. The following section is a brief summary of material covered in more detail in Charlie Trimm, "Causes of Genocide," in *The Cultural History of Genocide*, vol. 1: *The Ancient World*, ed. Tristan Taylor (London: Bloomsbury, 2021), 31–49.

19. Frank Chalk and Kurt Jonassohn, *The History and Sociology of Genocide: Analyses and Case Studies* (New Haven: Yale University Press, 1990), 61.

20. For details on these events, see Trimm, "Causes of Genocide," 31–36.

"considered them as inhabitants of Assyria."[21] However, this did not mean that the Assyrians sought to destroy the identity of these other groups. They had little interest in spreading the worship of Ashur as a religious deed or exterminating the worship of other gods. The Assyrian kings repaired cult centers of other gods in places outside of Assyria and allowed for the participation of the Assyrian king (usually by proxy) in rituals for non-Assyrian deities in those temples, thereby encouraging the continuation of group identity for these foreigners.[22] In a study of Assyrian influence in Philistine areas, Angelika Berlejung concludes, "A closer look only at Gaza and Ekron makes clear that there was not systematic and deliberate assyrianization or indoctrination of the West with Assyrian religion. The weapon of Ashur was not displayed in the West at all, no Assyrian temples were founded for the indigenous people, and anthropomorphic Assyrian divine statues are not attested at all."[23]

This same kind of attitude can be found elsewhere in the ancient Near East. The Hittites hated the Kasku to the north, but never campaigned to exterminate them. The Egyptians likewise disliked the Libyans to the west and the Nubians to the south, but did not seek to destroy them. One further observation from the divine combat myths helps to confirm this point, as the enemies in these myths (Tiamat, Apophis, Yam, Mot, etc.) were not gods of a foreign land.[24] The gods of foreign nations rather play the role of submissive and supportive

21. RINAP 1, 70.

22. Steven W. Holloway, *Aššur Is King! Aššur Is King! Religion in the Exercise of Power in the Neo-Assyrian Empire*, CHANE 10 (Leiden: Brill, 2002), 238–54, 261–68, 270–72.

23. Angelika Berlejung, "Shared Fates: Gaza and Ekron as Examples for the Assyrian Religious Policy in the West," in *Iconoclasm and Text Destruction in the Ancient Near East and Beyond*, ed. Natalie Naomi May, Oriental Institute Seminars 8 (Chicago: Oriental Institute, 2012), 167.

24. For a study of deities as opposed to monsters at Ugarit, see Mark S. Smith, "The Structure of Divinity at Ugarit and Israel: The Case of Anthropomorphic Deities versus Monstrous Divinities," in *Text, Artifact, and Image: Revealing Ancient Israelite Religion*, ed. Gary Beckman and Theodore J. Lewis, BJS 346 (Providence, RI: Brown Judaic Studies, 2006), 38–63.

allies: when a foreign nation was conquered their deity was seen as opposed to their peoples' rebellion from the beginning. In sum, the Assyrians and others in the ancient Near East did not view ethnicity or religion as a group identity to be destroyed by genocide.

One common feature of many of the stories of mass slaughter in the ancient Near East is rebellion: the powerful groups viewed rebellion as chaos threatening their control and sought to put it down as vigorously as possible (see the fight against chaos as a cause of war in chapter one). However, this does not mean that the Assyrians would seek to destroy that group entirely. As Carly Crouch says, "the primary object of warfare is not the destruction of the enemy but the destruction of it as opposed to Assyria."[25] Once the group submitted to the empire, then they were welcomed as Assyrians. The same approach can be seen in Egypt, where the most important identifying mark was one's attitude toward the pharaoh: "There is still no international legal basis for the distinction between outside and inside. Anyone who acknowledges Pharaoh is inside, regardless of whether he lives in Aleppo [a city outside of Egypt] or Asyut [a city in Egypt]; whoever disowns him is outside."[26]

The closest parallel to this in modern terms might be the political party criterion discussed above. As noted, this has been one of the controversial aspects of defining genocide since it was not included in the UN Convention on Genocide. While this might be the best way to find an event in the ancient Near East that matches the modern definition of genocide, it is still a loose fit at best because the animosity toward the group remained only while they were in a state of rebellion and disappeared once they were defeated. I conclude my broader discussion of the topic with this argument:

---

25. Carly L. Crouch, *War and Ethics in the Ancient Near East: Military Violence in Light of Cosmology and History*, BZAW 407 (Berlin: de Gruyter, 2009), 47.

26. Jan Assmann, "Zum Konzept der Fremdheit im alten Ägypten," in *Die Begegnung mit dem Fremden: Wertungen und Wirkungen in Hochkulturen vom Altertum bis zur Gegenwart*, ed. M. Schuster, Colloquium Rauricum 4 (Stuttgart: Teubner, 1996), 86. My translation; quotation originally in German.

It is most likely best to talk about mass killings in the ancient Near East in terms other than genocide because of the vast cultural gulf between our modern cultures and those in the ancient Near East. Referring to ancient Near Eastern events as genocide without qualification would most likely cause researchers to misunderstand the events because of the temptation to import the modern cultural ideas often associated with genocide into an ancient context. . . . However, this does not mean that we give the nations of the ancient Near East a free ethical pass because they did not commit "genocide," but the caution in identifying the events as genocide helps to clarify the categorization of events both in the study of the ancient Near East and in the history of genocide. [27]

However, while this statement might be true for the time period as a whole, the event in the ancient Near East that most closely parallels modern definitions of genocide is the destruction of the Canaanites. Therefore, we will now turn to examine the background of this event in more detail.

27. Trimm, "Causes of Genocide," 48–49.

Chapter Three

CANAANITES

The Origin and History of the Canaanites

Although these borders are not exact, the Canaanites were a group of people who lived in the land between the Mediterranean Sea on the west and the Jordan Rift (which includes the Sea of Galilee and the Dead Sea) on the east. The southern border was the desert area, while the northern boundary most likely included much of modern-day Lebanon.[1] Before the land was known as Canaan, Egyptians frequently called it "Retenu," while Mesopotamians called the entire region west of the Euphrates River "Amurru."[2] The name "Canaan" only began to appear in texts around the middle of the second millennium, such as the inscription found on the statue of a king named Idrimi from around the fifteenth century BCE.[3] The people of Ugarit, a city on the coast of the Mediterranean north of Canaan, used the term to describe a foreign merchant, distancing themselves from it—a perspective that complicates attempts to use the Ugaritic material as source material for Canaanite

1. Anson F. Rainey and R. Steven Notley, *The Sacred Bridge: Carta's Atlas of the Biblical World* (Jerusalem: Carta, 2006), 33–36.
2. Rainey and Notley, *Sacred Bridge*, 31–32.
3. Anson F. Rainey, "Who Is a Canaanite? A Review of the Textual Evidence," *BASOR* 304 (1996): 1–15. A Mari text refers to Canaanites in connection with "brigands" in the eighteenth century BCE, but it is not clear if they should be identified with the Canaanites near the Mediterranean; see Georges Dossin, "Une mention de Cananéens dans une lettre de Mari," *Syria* 50.3/4 (1973): 277–82.

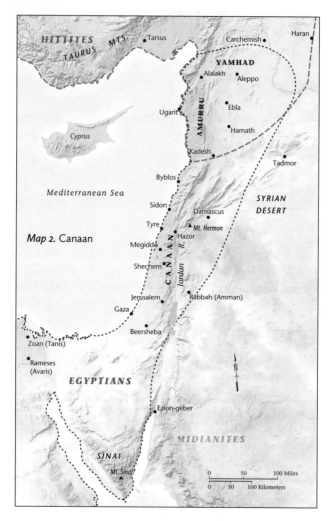

Map 2. Canaan

beliefs and practices.[4] "Canaanite" first appears in Egyptian texts in an inscription of Amenhotep II (around 1400 BCE), who recorded that he captured 640 Canaanites.[5] It also appears in an inscription from Mer-

4. Rainey, "Who Is a Canaanite?," 4–6.
5. "The Memphis and Karnak Stelae of Amenhotep II," trans. James K. Hoffmeier (COS 2.3:21).

neptah about a century later in the same text mentioned above that refers to the destruction of Israel: "Canaan is plundered."[6]

In the third millennium Canaan was connected through trade to Egypt and suffered occasional raids from its more powerful southern neighbor. In the early second millennium Canaan seems to have been ruled by powerful city-states, but came under increasing influence from Egypt. During the Second Intermediate Period in Egypt (1650–1560 BCE), the Hyksos, who temporarily ruled Egypt, might have been Canaanite in origin. However, with the rise of the New Kingdom pharaohs, especially Thutmose III (1479–1425 BCE), Canaan was progressively brought under the direct control of Egypt until Egypt weakened after 1200 BCE and the land of Canaan was restored to a greater level of independence from Egypt. However, by this time other groups like the Israelites, Moabites, and Ammonites had grown in power, and eventually the Canaanites disappeared.

Due to a lack of texts, we can only see hints of Canaanite culture outside of the Old Testament. The material from Ugarit is often drawn on as the primary source of Canaanite culture, but as noted above it needs to be remembered that Ugarit viewed Canaan as foreign. Therefore, caution must be used when appropriating this material.[7] The Amarna letters—letters written from Canaanites kings to Pharaoh Akhenaten around 1350 BCE—illustrate the overriding concern about military defeat (and even assassination attempts) of the elite Canaanites as they sought the help of the pharaoh. The political scene depicted in these letters involves many smaller city-states competing with each other for power and influence.

According to the Old Testament, the Canaanites came from Canaan, the son of Ham and grandson of Noah (Gen. 10:6). However, even before he appears in this genealogy Canaan is highlighted because of his role in the sordid story of Noah, the vineyard, and Noah's son Ham (Gen. 9:20–27). This story is obscure for a variety of reasons,

---

6. "The (Israel) Stela of Merneptah," trans. James K. Hoffmeier (*COS* 2.6:41).

7. For a summary of the material from Ugarit, see Mark S. Smith, "Ugarit and the Ugaritians," in *The World around the Old Testament*, ed. Bill T. Arnold and Brent A. Strawn (Grand Rapids: Baker, 2016), 139–67.

not least the difficulty in identifying what exactly Ham did that led to Noah's curse. The traditional understanding has been that Ham's sin was voyeurism—he merely saw his father naked—but many recent interpreters view his action as more serious based on the comment that Noah "knew what his youngest son had *done* to him" (Gen. 9:24). In addition, the phrase "uncover the nakedness" of a person frequently denotes sexual intercourse; most prominently, this phrase is repeated frequently in the sexual ethics chapter of Leviticus 18 where the misdeeds are described as those of the nations of Canaan and Egypt. Egypt was also a son of Ham and the nation of Egypt is sometimes referred to as Ham (Pss. 78:51; 105:23). Based on these hints, many now read the story as a sexual assault of Noah or Noah's wife.

However, this still does not explain why Noah curses Canaan rather than Ham (Gen. 9:25). Some possible rationales include the impossibility of cursing Ham since he had been previously blessed (Gen. 9:1) or the reciprocal breaking of the father-son relationship of Ham-Canaan as Ham broke his relationship with his own father. Some critical scholars see the entire story as a later justification for the Israelite oppression of the Canaanites. A further disturbing possibility is based on the reference in the quotation above about "what his *youngest son* had done to him." Ham is always listed as the second son of Noah, not the youngest son (Gen. 5:32; 6:10; 7:13; 9:18; 10:1; 1 Chron. 1:4). However, Canaan is listed as the youngest son of Ham (Gen. 10:6; 1 Chron. 1:8), perhaps indicating that Canaan receives the curse because he was actually the one who committed the sexual assault. Regardless of whether one follows this interpretation or the traditional reading, the Old Testament introduction to Canaan begins on a low note.

After this introduction, the Canaanites are listed in two ways. The first is couched in terms of the descendants of Canaan: "Canaan fathered Sidon his firstborn and Heth, and the Jebusites, the Amorites, the Girgashites, the Hivites, the Arkites, the Sinites, the Arvadites, the Zemarites, and the Hamathites. Afterward the clans of the Canaanites dispersed" (Gen. 10:15–18). More commonly, the Canaanites are lumped in with other groups who inhabit the land of Canaan: "On that day the LORD made a covenant with Abram, saying, 'To your offspring I give this land, from the river of Egypt to the great river, the river Euphrates, the land of the Kenites, the Kenizzites, the Kadmonites, the Hittites, the Perizzites, the Rephaim, the Amorites, the Canaanites, the Girgashites and the Jebusites'" (Gen. 15:18–21).

The relationship between the Canaanites and these other groups is not clear. In some cases the Canaanites seem to be one group among many: "The Amalekites dwell in the land of the Negeb. The Hittites, the Jebusites, and the Amorites dwell in the hill country. And the Canaanites dwell by the sea, and along the Jordan" (Num. 13:29). A similar connection of the Amorites with the hill country and the Canaanites with the land near the sea is found in Deuteronomy 1:7.[8] However, in other cases the term "Canaanite" seems to refer to all of the groups living in the area, especially in light of the listing of these groups as descendants of Canaan (Gen. 10:15–18) and the constant use of the phrase "land of Canaan." The reference to Esau's wives highlights this, as they are collectively called Canaanites, but then one wife is described as Hittite and the other as Hivite (Gen. 36:2).

Both Joshua and Judges make clear that Israel was only able to conquer part of the land of Canaan, as the battles were mainly focused on the highlands and Galilee. Most of Canaan, and especially the valuable land closest to the international highway that ran along the coast and through the Jezreel Valley, remained in Canaanite hands (Josh. 15:63; 16:10; 17:12–13; 19:47; Judg. 1). Judges records that conflict occasionally arose with local Canaanites, such as the battle against Jabin, a Canaanite king based at Hazor (Judg. 4). It was only under the reign of David and Solomon that these areas were brought under full Israelite control (1 Kings 9:16–21). During the early first millennium the term "Canaanite" dropped out of use and became a historical term rather than a way to refer to contemporary inhabitants of Canaan.[9] The use of "Canaanite" in Matthew 15:22 is most likely designed to

8. The connection between the Amorites in the Bible and the Amorites of Mesopotamia is unclear; for a discussion see Daniel E. Fleming, "The Amorites," in *The World around the Old Testament*, ed. Bill T. Arnold and Brent A. Strawn (Grand Rapids: Baker Academic, 2016), 1–30.

9. Katell Berthelot, "Where May Canaanites Be Found? Canaanites, Phoenicians, and Others in Jewish Texts from the Hellenistic and Roman Periods," in *The Gift of the Land and the Fate of the Canaanites in Jewish Thought*, ed. Katell

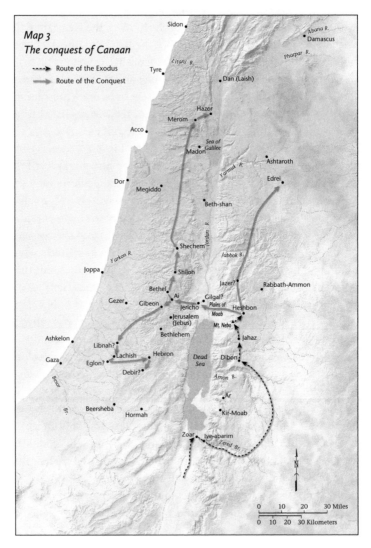

Map 3
The conquest of Canaan

- - - - ▶ Route of the Exodus
━━━▶ Route of the Conquest

Sidon

Abana R.
Damascus

Pharpar R.

Tyre

Litani R.

Dan (Laish)

Hazor

Merom

Acco

Sea of Galilee

Madon

Yarmuk R.

Ashtaroth

Dor

Megiddo

Edrei

Beth-shan

Jordan R.

Shechem

Jabbok R.

Joppa

Yarkon R.

Shiloh

Jazer?

Rabbath-Ammon

Bethel

Ai

Gilgal?

Gezer

Gibeon

Jericho

Plains of Moab

Heshbon

Jerusalem
(Jebus)

Mt. Nebo

Bethlehem

Jahaz

Ashkelon

Libnah?

Lachish

Hebron

Dead Sea

Dibon

Gaza

Eglon?

Debir?

Besor Br.

Arnon R.

Ar

Beersheba

Hormah

Kir-Moab

Zoar

Iye-abarim

Zered Br.

N

| 0 | 10 | 20 | 30 Miles |
| 0 | 10 | 20 | 30 Kilometers |

force the reader to think in Old Testament terms as this would be an unnatural way to refer to someone in New Testament times.

Berthelot, Joseph E. David, and Marc Hirshman (Oxford: Oxford University Press, 2014), 253–74.

The Commanded Treatment of the Canaanites

The book of Genesis presents a mixed perspective on the Canaanites. On the one hand, the patriarchs have a positive relationship with the Canaanites. While his main motivation is to rescue Lot, Abraham also rescues the Amorites and their possessions that have been taken by the eastern kings (Gen. 14). Later he buys a field from Canaanites for what appears to be a very high price (Gen. 23), Judah marries a Canaanite woman (Gen. 38:2), and Joseph is instrumental in rescuing not only the Egyptians from famine, but also the Canaanites (Gen. 47:13–22). On the other hand, Genesis also exhibits tensions between the patriarchs and the Canaanites. YHWH says to Abraham that his descendants "shall come back here [Canaan] in the fourth generation, for the iniquity of the Amorites is not yet complete" (Gen. 15:16). Isaac refused to allow Jacob to marry a Canaanite (Gen. 27:46–28:9), and Jacob's sons decimate the Canaanite town of Shechem (Gen. 34).

The possibility of the Israelites inhabiting the land of Canaan as a large people rather than as a family first appears in the early chapters of Exodus (3:8, 17; 6:4; 13:5, 11), but no reference is made at that point as to what the Israelites should do in regard to the Canaanites. The Song of the Sea, which Moses and the people sang to YHWH when he delivered them from the Egyptians at the Red Sea, refers to the inhabitants of Canaan melting away in fear of the Israelites (Exod. 15:15). However, the first extended set of instructions for interacting with the Canaanites comes in the Covenant Code (Exod. 23:23–30), as YHWH promises that his angel and his terror (similar to the brilliance of the Assyrians mentioned in chapter one) will go before Israel, that he will cause the Canaanites to disappear, and that the "hornet" will banish the Canaanites (see table 1 for more details on these phrases). However, this expulsion will only be gradual. The Israelites' responsibility is to destroy Canaanite religious items, make no covenant with the Canaanite peoples, and banish them.

In Leviticus 18:24–30, YHWH's promise to drive out the Canaanites is similar to the Exodus text but employs a different word (see table 1). In addition, the Leviticus passage claims that the land itself will vomit out the inhabitants due to their sin. The only responsibility of the Israelites is to follow YHWH. The next text, Numbers 33:50–56, focuses more on the responsibility of the Israelites, as YHWH promises very little. Instead, the Israelites are to drive out the Canaanites, following the concept presented in the previous texts, but using yet another different word (see table 1). They are also to destroy Canaanite religious items and take possession of the land.

The final set of texts about the Canaanites comes in Deuteronomy. The commands in Deuteronomy 6:18–19 sound similar to what we have seen in the previous passages, as YHWH promises to give the land to Israel and instructs Israel to push out the Canaanites. However, Deuteronomy 7:1–5 includes a new note. Although YHWH reiterated his promise to clear away the Canaanites (similar to the previous ideas about expulsion, but using yet again a different word) and give the Canaanites to Israel, Israel's primary instruction is to put the Canaanites to *herem*.[10] The word *herem* occurs rarely outside of the Old Testament. It appears in a south Arabian text from around 700 BCE which includes many parallels with Joshua: extensive destruction, the killing of many people, a city opened up for settlement, and the creation of a cultic installation.[11] However, the closest parallel is from around 850 BCE in Moabite—a language very similar to Hebrew. Mesha, a Moabite king mentioned in the Old Testament (2 Kings 3:4), declared that at Nebo he "slew all of them [Israelites], seven thousand men and boys and women and girls and maidens because I had dedicated it [put it to *herem*] to ʿAštār-Kəmôš [the Moabite deity]."[12]

10. For an introduction to the secondary literature on this term, see Philip D. Stern, *The Biblical* Herem: *A Window on Israel's Religious Experience*, BJS 211 (Atlanta: Scholars Press, 1991); Susan Niditch, *War in the Hebrew Bible: A Study in the Ethics of Violence* (New York: Oxford University Press, 1993), 28–77; K. Lawson Younger Jr., "Some Recent Discussion on the *Herem*," in *Far from Minimal: Celebrating the Work and Influence of Philip R. Davies*, ed. Duncan Burns and J. W. Rogerson (New York: T&T Clark, 2012), 505–22; Charlie Trimm, "Recent Research on Warfare in the Old Testament," *CBR* 10 (2012): 9–10.

11. Lauren A. S. Monroe, "Israelite, Moabite and Sabaean War-*Herem* Traditions and the Forging of National Identity: Reconsidering the Sabaean Text RES 3945 in Light of Biblical and Moabite Evidence," *VT* 57 (2007): 335.

12. Shmuel Ahituv, *Echoes from the Past: Hebrew and Cognate Inscriptions from the Biblical Period* (Jerusalem: Carta, 2008), 394.

Table 1

	Exodus 23:23–30	Leviticus 18:24–30	Numbers 33:50–56	Deuteronomy 6:18–19	Deuteronomy 7:1–5
YHWH	1. Angel and terror go ahead of Israel 2. Causes Canaanites to disappear 3. Throws Canaanites into confusion 4. Hornet banishes (*giresh*) the Canaanites	1. Drives out (*shileh*) the Canaanites	1. Gives the land to Israel	1. Gives the land to Israel	1. Clears away (*nashal*) the Canaanites 2. Gives the Canaanites to Israel
Israel	1. Destroys Canaanite religious items 2. Makes no covenant with the Canaanites 3. Banishes (*giresh*) the Canaanites	1. Is not to act like the Canaanites	1. Drives out (*yarash*) the Canaanites 2. Destroys Canaanite religious items 3. Takes possession (*yarash*) of the land	1. Takes possession of the land 2. Pushes out (*hadaf*) the Canaanites	1. Strikes the Canaanites 2. *Herem* (*haherim*) the Canaanites 3. Makes no covenant with the Canaanites 4. No intermarriage with the Canaanites 5. Destroys Canaanite religious items
Land		1. Vomits out the Canaanites			

In the Old Testament, this word is used in a variety of ways.[13] First, *herem* is a punishment for Israelite idolaters: "Whoever sacrifices to any god, other than the LORD alone, shall be devoted to destruction [put to *herem*]" (Exod. 22:20). While this verse does not provide any context for understanding the specific nature of the word, the other reference to its application against Israelite idolaters is clearer since it is used in connection with putting them all to the sword and burning the city (Deut. 13:12–16). This is also one of the few places where an explicit connection is made between *herem* and sacrifice, as the burning of the city is called a "whole burnt offering." Second, the word *herem* is also used to denote gifts given to priests. One reference simply says to the priests that "every devoted thing [*herem*] in Israel shall be yours" (Num. 18:14). More detail is provided in Leviticus 27:21–29, where land and other kinds of property could be given to the priests as devoted gifts (*herem*), who could then use it.

Third, the most common use of *herem* is in military contexts against the Canaanites, first occurring in a battle against the Canaanite city of Arad (Num. 21:1–3). The next reference to *herem* occurs in the defeat of the Amorite kings Sihon and Og on the east side of the Jordan River as recorded in Deuteronomy (the parallel accounts in Numbers do not use this word). These accounts provide more background, as the word is used in connection with the phrase "we left no survivors" (Deut. 2:34). In addition, the fate of the men, women, and children who are put to *herem* is contrasted with the livestock and spoils that are kept as plunder (Deut. 3:6–7). However, these phrases about killing may not necessarily define *herem* and could represent distinct concepts from it.

The background of *herem* has been explained in different ways. Due to its appearance outside of Israel, it does not seem to be an Israelite invention. Philip Stern argues the *herem* was seen as a way to bring order in the face of chaos.[14] Tracy Lemos has suggested that the

---

13. The word most commonly appears either as a noun (*herem*) or as a causative verb (put something to *herem*).

14. Stern, *Biblical* Herem, 217–26.

mass killing by Mesha (and perhaps some of the genocidal language of Israel) was due to scarcity of land and resources.[15] Drawing on the use of the word in the Mesha Stela and the south Arabian text, Lauren Monroe makes a case for seeing *herem* as part of early state formation by showing a contrast between the empires and the smaller nations in their infancy: the empires did not wipe out nations because they were large enough to employ prisoners effectively, while the smaller nations instead wiped out other nations so as to appropriate their land for their own people.[16]

When the Israelites are first commanded to put the Canaanites to *herem* (Deut. 7:1–5; 20:16–17), the text confuses the matter by immediately including prohibitions against making covenants with the Canaanites, showing mercy to them, and intermarrying with them (Deut. 7:2–3). This discontinuity plays an important role in the discussion about the ethics of *herem*, leading some to argue that *herem* is a metaphorical denunciation that does not necessitate actual killing. Another possibility, based on its use only with cities in Joshua and in Deuteronomy 20, is that *herem* was only for the Canaanites in cities; the prohibition against intermarriage was then still relevant for the Canaanites in rural areas.[17]

When we turn to Joshua, the actual actions of the Israelites are divided between killing and expulsion. The main focus is on death

15. T. M. Lemos, "Dispossessing Nations: Population Growth, Scarcity, and Genocide in Ancient Israel and Twentieth-Century Rwanda," in *Ritual Violence in the Hebrew Bible: New Perspectives*, ed. Saul M. Olyan (Oxford: Oxford University Press, 2015), 27–66. However, a recent study suggests that these kinds of factors have not influenced cases of genocide in recent history (Hollie Nyseth Brehm, "Re-Examining Risk Factors of Genocide," *Journal of Genocide Research* 19 [2017]: 61–87).

16. Lauren A. S. Monroe, *Josiah's Reform and the Dynamics of Defilement: Israelite Rites of Violence and the Making of a Biblical Text* (Oxford: Oxford University Press, 2011), 45–56.

17. Markus Zehnder, "The Annihilation of the Canaanites: Reassessing the Brutality of the Biblical Witnesses," in *Encountering Violence in the Bible*, ed. Markus Zehnder and Hallvard Hagelia, The Bible in the Modern World 55 (Sheffield: Sheffield Phoenix, 2013), 273.

and destruction, with Jericho as the primary example of a city put under *herem* at the edge of the sword while only Rahab and her family are said to be left alive (Josh. 6:17, 21). In addition, Ai and many other cities are put to *herem* (Josh. 8:26; 10:28–40) and such phrases as "by the sword" and "left none remaining" are connected to *herem* (Josh. 10:28). The punishment of *herem* is also applied to an Israelite, Achan, who takes plunder from Jericho that has been declared *herem*, and is killed. This sets up a precedent for later Israelites to remember that YHWH would judge Israelites as he judged the Canaanites if they acted like Canaanites (Josh. 22:20).

However, in a few places the Israelites are said to expel Canaanites. Caleb banishes (*yarash*) the sons of Anak (Josh. 15:14; Judg. 1:20), and YHWH is also said to have banished (*giresh*, Josh. 24:18; Judg. 6:9) and driven out (*yarash*, Judg. 11:23; 1 Kings 14:24) the Canaanites. One later text emphasizes the parallel between Israel and Canaan by describing YHWH's action as sending Canaan into exile, a common phrase used to denote YHWH's judgment of Israel (2 Kings 17:11). As we will see in chapter six, this expulsion plays an important role in some defenses of the ethics of *herem*.

Finally, some see a connection between the Canaanites and the Nephilim of Genesis 6:4. Although the Nephilim are mentioned elsewhere only in the spies' report that they have seen the Nephilim in the land of Canaan (Num. 13:33), the spies also identify these Nephilim as the sons of Anak, who are mentioned in several places as living in the land of Canaan (Num. 13:22; Deut. 9:2; Josh. 11:21–22; 14:12). Based on this connection, Michael Heiser argues that the reason for the Canaanite destruction "was the specific elimination of the descendants of the Nephilim."[18] However, the Old Testament does not state this as a reason for the destruction of the Canaanites, and the killing of the non-Nephilim Canaanites remains a moral problem.

18. Michael S. Heiser, *The Unseen Realm: Recovering the Supernatural Worldview of the Bible* (Bellingham, WA: Lexham, 2015), 210–11.

PART TWO

YHWH and the Destruction of the Canaanites

∾

Chapter Four

REEVALUATING GOD

Four Possible Views

Having laid a foundation for our conversation about the Canaanite problem, we can now begin our journey through the various proposals about how to deal with the problem. For the sake of organization, it will be best to arrange the proposals into categories that will help us to compare and contrast them, even though one must always remember that each scholar has their own particular understanding of the problem.[1] I will arrange the proposals according to the following four propositions.[2]

1.   God is good and compassionate.
2.   The Old Testament is a faithful record of God's dealings with humanity and favorably portrays YHWH's actions.

1. For the most part, the scholars quoted in Part Two specialize in Old Testament studies, though some work in fields like philosophy and theology.

2. For others who have framed the problem with similar questions, see Randal Rauser, "'Let Nothing That Breathes Remain Alive': On the Problem of Divinely Commanded Genocide," *Philosophia Christi* 11 (2009): 28–29; Christian Hofreiter, *Making Sense of Old Testament Genocide: Christian Interpretations of Herem Passages*, Oxford Theology and Religion Monographs (Oxford: Oxford University Press, 2018), 9; Webb and Oeste, *Bloody, Brutal, and Barbaric*, 19–21. Various other surveys of this topic have been written; for example, a sevenfold structure is found in Eric A. Seibert, "Recent Research on Divine Violence in the Old Testament (with Special Attention to Christian Theological Perspectives)," *CBR* 15 (2016): 8–40.

3. The Old Testament describes events that are similar to genocide.
4. Mass killings are always evil.

All four of these propositions cannot be true at the same time because of the contradictions between them. Therefore, as an entry point into recent discussions, this part of the book will evaluate the various proposals on how to deal with the problem of the destruction of the Canaanites on the basis of which these four propositions are denied.

1. Reevaluating God (this chapter): God is not good.
2. Reevaluating the Old Testament (chapter five): the Old Testament is not a faithful record.
3. Reevaluating the Interpretation of the Old Testament (chapter six): the Old Testament does not describe anything like a genocide.
4. Reevaluating Violence in the Old Testament (chapter seven): the mass killing of the Canaanites in the Old Testament was permitted for that one point in history.

Several of the key differences between the various views are listed in table 2.

Table 2

	View 1	View 2	View 3	View 4
Does the Old Testament depict mass killing beyond normal military battles?	Yes	Yes	No	Yes
Should readers accept the violent portions of the Old Testament?	No	No	Yes	Yes
Should readers accept the Bible in general?	No	Yes	Yes	Yes

Overview of View 1

We will begin with what is in many ways the simplest solution: reject the belief that God is good and worthy to be followed. This is not a new path, but represents a critique of Christianity from as long ago as Celsus in the second century CE, who highlighted the contradiction between the God of Moses who commanded the slaughter of an entire race with the command of Jesus to turn the other cheek.[3]

More recently, this view has been popularized by the New Atheists, as illustrated by the following representative quotation from Richard Dawkins: "The God of the Old Testament is arguably the most unpleasant character in all fiction: jealous and proud of it; a petty, unjust, unforgiving control-freak; a vindictive, bloodthirsty ethnic cleanser; a misogynistic, homophobic, racist, infanticidal, genocidal, filicidal, pestilential, megalomaniacal, sadomasochistic, capriciously malevolent bully."[4]

Dan Barker, a former evangelical pastor who has walked away from the faith, wrote an entire book based on this quotation called *God: The Most Unpleasant Character in All Fiction*.[5] Hector Avalos studied the origins of religious violence and concluded the following: "Since all religious beliefs are ultimately unverifiable, the greatest scarce resource of all is verifiability. And one way to remedy or minimize unverifiability in any decision-making process, especially that leading to violence, is to eliminate religion from human life alto-

---

3. His works survive only in the response by Origen; for a summary, see Hofreiter, *Making Sense of Old Testament Genocide*, 79–85. For a historical survey of those who have rejected the God of the Bible because of his connection with violence, see Philip Jenkins, *Laying Down the Sword: Why We Can't Ignore the Bible's Violent Verses* (New York: HarperOne, 2011), 167–82.

4. Richard Dawkins, *The God Delusion* (Boston: Mariner, 2006), 51.

5. Dan Barker, *God: The Most Unpleasant Character in All Fiction* (New York: Sterling, 2016).

gether."[6] In sum, the divine violence in the Old Testament leads these scholars to reject the whole package of monotheism.[7]

Summary

The benefit of this view is that it clearly solves the problem of divine violence by simply rejecting the deity wholesale. However, the cost is also clear: the rejection of the entire notion of monotheism has severe social and existential costs for many. For those who had previously claimed faith, their social circles will be extensively disrupted and friendships lost. The faith that had previously provided a foundation for life will also be lost. In ethical terms, new grounds besides theism will need to be acquired to serve as a foundation for ethics and morality. For example, if religion previously provided the grounds for rejecting genocide as evil—perhaps on the basis of the dignity provided to humans as the image of God—then other grounds will need to be found to establish the value of human life and hence the depravity of genocide.

6. See Hector Avalos, *Fighting Words: The Origins of Religious Violence* (Amherst, NY: Prometheus, 2005), 371. For another recent defense of this view, see Evan Fales, "Satanic Verses: Moral Chaos in the Holy Writ," in *Divine Evil? The Moral Character of the God of Abraham*, ed. Michael Bergmann, Michael J. Murray, and Michael C. Rea (Oxford: Oxford University Press, 2011), 91–108.

7. For the argument that monotheism is the foundation of violence, see Regina Schwartz, *The Curse of Cain: The Violent Legacy of Monotheism* (Chicago: University of Chicago Press, 1997).

Chapter Five

REEVALUATING THE OLD TESTAMENT

Overview of View 2

A second group solves the problem by reevaluating the statement that the Old Testament is a faithful record of God's interaction with humans. They argue that while the Old Testament records examples of extreme divine violence, we should not accept those violent texts as authoritative for us and should disassociate God from them. Many examples of disconnecting authors from their earlier work are known in recent history, such as Hergé, the creator of the internationally popular Tintin series. His early work was filled with racism, especially in *Tintin in the Congo*. As part of an effective marketing technique, the back cover of each Tintin book includes pictures of the covers of all the other Tintin books. However, most English translations of Tintin do not include the cover of the racist *Tintin in the Congo*, effectively removing it from the Tintin "canon." More famously, the 1946 Disney film *Song of the South* has been repudiated because of its racism and was not included in the streaming catalog of Disney+, making it very difficult to watch today. In both of these examples, the proposed way forward was to reject the offending book or movie but preserve Tintin or Disney as a whole. The scholars who adhere to this view seek to do something similar with the Old Testament: disavow the offensive portions but keep the Old Testament as a part of the Bible.

Historicity

One of the most common ways of disavowing the violent events is to argue that they never happened. Many Old Testament scholars reject the historicity of the events of Joshua, believing that these texts should not be read as historical accounts. Instead, they ascribe the creation of these violent texts to much later in Judean history, such as the time of Josiah and his attempts to reform Judah by removing the remnants of Canaanite religion (2 Kings 22:1–23:30).[1] In other words, they claim not only that these stories were written many centuries after they were purported to have happened but also that they were written as fictional accounts to defend the political positions of Josiah. For Kenton Sparks, this is comforting because the focus is Canaanite religion rather than the Canaanite people, who no longer existed at the time of Josiah: "So the author of Deuteronomy—who elsewhere defended the cause of widows, orphans, and aliens—was a far softer fellow than the genocide texts suggest."[2] Other scholars date these violent texts even later than the time of Josiah. Rüdiger Schmitt views the majority of the warfare material in the Old Testament as originating from the exilic and postexilic times and having little to do with actual warfare, serving instead as a metaphor for keeping the law.[3] Yair Hoffman even counter-intuitively suggests that the *herem* laws were largely created in the postexilic period to argue that the

---

1. For example, see Yoshihide Suzuki, "A New Aspect of *Hrm* in Deuteronomy in View of an Assimilation Policy of King Josiah," *Annual of the Japanese Biblical Institute* 21 (1995): 3–27; Lori L. Rowlett, *Joshua and the Rhetoric of Violence: A New Historicist Analysis*, JSOTSup 226 (Sheffield: Sheffield Academic, 1996); Temba L. J. Mafico, "Joshua," in *The Africana Bible: Reading Israel's Scriptures from Africa and the African Diaspora*, ed. Hugh R. Page Jr. (Minneapolis: Fortress, 2010), 115–19. For the dating of the *herem* texts to the reign of Jeroboam II, see Stern, *Biblical* Herem.

2. Kenton L. Sparks, *Sacred Word, Broken Word: Biblical Authority and the Dark Side of Scripture* (Grand Rapids: Eerdmans, 2012), 112. For similar thoughts, see Peter Enns, *The Bible Tells Me So: Why Defending Scripture Has Made Us Unable to Read It* (New York: HarperOne, 2014), 58–60.

3. Rüdiger Schmitt, *Der "Heilige Krieg" im Pentateuch und im deuteronomistischen Geschichtswerk: Studien zur Forschungs-, Rezeptions- und Reli-*

Jews should *accept* foreigners: according to the mythic history of the destruction of the Canaanites they no longer existed and therefore foreigners presented no further danger.[4]

Rejecting the historicity of the violent texts neatly solves the problem at a certain level, although it remains problematic that the ancient writers of the Old Testament would create stories like this and think that YHWH would speak in such a fashion. As Regina Schwartz says, "We need to take the ethics of these stories seriously because such stories are the cultural locus where, if anywhere, ethics are encoded."[5] The following parable illustrates the problem with viewing the lack of historicity as the solution to the ethical problem.

> Suppose the older children in a family tell the younger children horrifying stories about how their father severely beats them for unmannerly behavior; and suppose that they also tell stories according to which the father insisted that they be willing to sell themselves into prostitution in order to help pay the family bills. Now imagine the older kids later saying, "Our stories weren't meant to be taken as 'history'. Their basic message is that good manners and helping to pull one's own weight in the family are important to our father. We simply exaggerated a lot to make the point." Most of us would think that, on the assumption that *some* of the younger kids *might* believe the stories just as they are told, what the older kids have done here is utterly appalling. And matters are made worse, not better, by the supposition that the father himself inspired or otherwise authorized the telling of these stories as his "revelation" to his younger children. No decent father would do such a thing.[6]

gionsgeschichte von Krieg und Bann im Alten Testament, AOAT 381 (Münster: Ugarit-Verlag, 2011).

4. Yair Hoffman, "The Deuteronomistic Concept of the *Herem*," *ZAW* 111 (1999): 196–210.

5. Schwartz, *Curse of Cain*, 62. See also John J. Collins, "The God of Joshua," *SJOT* 28 (2014): 212–28.

6. Michael Bergmann, Michael Murray, and Michael Rea, "Introduction," in *Divine Evil? The Moral Character of the God of Abraham*, ed. Michael Bergmann,

Innate Human Ethics

Another way to reevaluate the Old Testament is to reject the violent stories of the Old Testament on ethical grounds rather than historical grounds. In other words, we intuitively know that genocide is evil, therefore we should reject accounts of genocide even when they appear in sacred texts.[7] Randal Rauser compiles four ethical reasons why these violent actions cannot be attributed to YHWH: (1) killing babies is bad, (2) slaughter causes damage to the soldiers, (3) the account fits the description of other genocides (it is not an extraordinary exception), and (4) the Canaanite genocide has led to other genocides.[8] Likewise, John Collins wants readers to recognize that the Bible "is no infallible guide on ethical matters."[9] In other words, our innate ethical sense should guide us to reject the extreme violence in the Old Testament. Some scholars have identified the ethical censoring of violent tendencies even within the Old Testament itself by arguing that later editors sought to tone down the violence of warfare texts. For example, Thomas Römer argues that, according to Josiah, the God of the conquest was a warrior God, but later during the Babylonian exile editors demilitarized the war stories; for example, Joshua 1:8 changed Joshua from a military leader to a rabbi.[10] A counterargument is that this is a human-centered view that disregards the divine inspiration of Scripture. In addition, to be consistent

---

Michael Murray, and Michael Rea (Oxford: Oxford University Press, 2011), 9–10. Italics in original.

7. Eryl W. Davies, *The Immoral Bible: Approaches to Biblical Ethics* (T&T Clark, 2010), 120–38.

8. Rauser, "'Let Nothing That Breathes Remain Alive.'"

9. John J. Collins, *Does the Bible Justify Violence?*, Facets (Minneapolis: Fortress Press, 2004), 32.

10. Thomas Römer, *Dark God: Cruelty, Sex, and Violence in the Old Testament*, trans. Sean O'Neill (New York: Paulist, 2013), 76–86. For other arguments for a toning down of the violence by later editors, see Lawson G. Stone, "Ethical and Apologetic Tendencies in the Redaction of the Book of Joshua," *CBQ* 53 (1991): 25–35.

significant portions of both testaments would need to be rejected due to the violence in the New Testament.

Misunderstanding

Another approach within this view is based on the idea of misunderstanding: Israel went beyond what God wanted them to do. Walter Brueggemann argues that God's main command concerning the Canaanites is that given in Joshua 11:6, which is restricted to hamstringing the horses and destroying the chariots of the Canaanites. Israel is not to have its own army, but to trust God. The only violence commanded by God is violence against weapons, not by weapons. According to Brueggemann, "One may imagine that Israel took that limited, disciplined warrant of Yahweh and went well beyond its intent or substance in its action, out of rage and oppression."[11] In other words, Israel's destruction of the Canaanites was not what God desired. Likewise, Thom Stark says, "My contention is that God never did command the Israelites to slaughter entire peoples wholesale. These accounts reflect a standard imperialistic ideology that Israel shared with many of its ancient neighbors, and I read them as products of ancient culture, not as products of pure divine revelation."[12] A similar approach is to employ a relativism of blame model: "Moral ignorance that is owing to one's cultural or historical position is nonculpable."[13] However, a significant problem for this approach is that the Old Testament does not record any rebuke from God about the

11. Walter Brueggemann, *Divine Presence Amid Violence: Contextualizing the Book of Joshua* (Eugene, OR: Cascade, 2009), 39.

12. Thom Stark, *The Human Faces of God: What Scripture Reveals When It Gets God Wrong (and Why Inerrancy Tries to Hide It)* (Eugene, OR: Wipf & Stock, 2011), 150.

13. Miranda Fricker, "The Relativism of Blame and Williams' Relativism of Distance," *Proceedings of the Aristotelian Society Supplementary* 84 (2010): 167. I thank J. Blair Wilgus for bringing this article to my attention.

Israelites misunderstanding him and the conquest is presented as an important part of God's plan for the world.[14]

Christology

One of the more popular methods used by those who fall into view 2 is to read the Old Testament Christocentrically. According to the New Testament, Jesus is the ultimate image of God. Therefore, if we want to know what God is like, then we should look at Jesus. Since Jesus is nonviolent as portrayed in the Gospels, then following this method teaches us that God himself is pacifistic and the violence attributed to YHWH in the Old Testament must be mistaken in some way. C. S. Cowles argues "that a radical shift in the understanding of God's character and the sanctity of all human life occurred in between the days of the first Joshua and the second Joshua (i.e., Jesus) is beyond dispute."[15] In the same way that Jesus updates the divorce command originally given by Moses, he also updates the genocide commands.[16]

The most well-known advocate of this position is Eric Seibert, who argues that "God's moral character is most clearly and completely revealed through the person of Jesus."[17] Instead of commanding the destruction of foreigners, Jesus reveals to us a God who is nonviolent and kind to the wicked.[18] If an Old Testament text does not match this nonviolent image of Jesus, then it should be rejected. Derek Flood offers another New Testament–centered view when he

14. Christopher J. H. Wright, *The God I Don't Understand: Reflections on Tough Questions of Faith* (Grand Rapids: Zondervan, 2008), 82–83.

15. C. S. Cowles, "The Case for Radical Discontinuity," in *Show Them No Mercy: Four Views on God and Canaanite Genocide* (Grand Rapids: Zondervan, 2003), 41.

16. Cowles, "Case for Radical Discontinuity," 33–34. See also J. Denny Weaver, *The Nonviolent God* (Grand Rapids: Eerdmans, 2013).

17. Eric A. Seibert, *Disturbing Divine Behavior: Troubling Old Testament Images of God* (Minneapolis: Fortress, 2009), 185.

18. Seibert, *Disturbing Divine Behavior*, 190–203.

argues that Jesus and Paul repudiate the violence of the Old Testament through such tactics as selective quotation. In his view, Jesus replaces the retributive justice of the Old Testament with restorative justice. We should read the Old Testament with an attitude of "faithful questioning" rather than "unquestioning obedience."[19] Richard Hays states his opinion even more bluntly: "If irreconcilable tensions exist between the moral vision of the New Testament and that of particular Old Testament texts, the New Testament vision trumps the Old Testament. . . . Everything is changed by the cross and resurrection."[20]

Gregory Boyd advocates for a similar view, as seen in the subtitle of his book: *Interpreting the Old Testament's Violent Portraits of God in Light of the Cross*. Since he follows a theological interpretation of Scripture and what he calls the "conservative hermeneutical principle," he is uncomfortable with merely rejecting portions of the Old Testament.[21] However, he still sees the nonviolent life and ministry of Jesus, culminating in the cross, as determinative for understanding the Old Testament. His interpretation of divine violence is that it is not a direct act of God, but God removing his protective hand and allowing evil forces (often cosmic) to act violently against humans, causing sin to self-destruct.[22] Evidence for this can easily be found in the Old Testament, such as YHWH employing Assyria as a tool against Israel (Isa. 10:5). However, many cases of divine-ordained violence are executed by prophets and other followers of YHWH; Boyd accounts for this as a result of God not micromanaging the use of

19. Derek Flood, *Disarming Scripture: Cherry-Picking Liberals, Violence-Loving Conservatives, and Why We All Need to Learn to Read the Bible Like Jesus Did* (San Francisco: Metanoia, 2014), 23–70.

20. Richard B. Hays, *The Moral Vision of the New Testament: A Contemporary Introduction to New Testament Ethics* (San Francisco: HarperCollins, 1996), 336–37.

21. Gregory A. Boyd, *Crucifixion of the Warrior God: Interpreting the Old Testament's Violent Portraits of God in Light of the Cross*, 2 vols. (Minneapolis: Fortress, 2017), 513–52.

22. Boyd, *Crucifixion of the Warrior God*, 768.

his gifts.[23] When it comes to the destruction of the Canaanites, Boyd argues that YHWH's original plan was for a nonviolent conquest.[24] While Boyd can find many examples to support his view of divine violence, his desire to fit every single case of divine violence into his paradigm seems to many as an injustice to the text. This is especially the case when his view forces him into positions like saying that the tenth plague (the death of the firstborn) and the ark of the covenant (connected with violent attacks against the Philistines in 1 Sam. 5) were both demonic.[25]

One problem with the Christological approach to violent texts in the Old Testament is the ghost of Marcion hovering in the background. Marcion of Sinope was a bishop in the early church who was declared a heretic because he rejected the Old Testament and large portions of the New Testament.[26] Tertullian summarizes Marcion's view of the contrast between the god of the Old Testament and the god of the New Testament in this way: "One judicial, harsh, mighty in war; the other mild, placid, and simply good and excellent."[27] Scholars who follow the Christological approach generally seek to distance themselves from Marcion by arguing that they still value the Old Testament when read correctly, whereas Marcion rejected it entirely.[28]

---

23. Boyd, *Crucifixion of the Warrior God*, 1196. For a similar argument about God using agents to whom he also gives freedom, see Terence E. Fretheim, "Violence and the God of the Old Testament," in *Encountering Violence in the Bible*, ed. Markus Zehnder and Hallvard Hagelia, The Bible in the Modern World 55 (Sheffield: Sheffield Phoenix, 2013), 116–20.

24. Boyd, *Crucifixion of the Warrior God*, 961–1002.

25. Boyd, *Crucifixion of the Warrior God*, 1178–83, 1231–47.

26. For more on Marcion, see Heikki Räisänen, "Marcion," in *A Companion to Second-Century Christian "Heretics,"* ed. Antti Marjanen and Petri Luomanen, VCSup 76 (Leiden: Brill, 2005), 100–124; Sebastian Moll, *The Arch-Heretic Marcion*, WUNT 250 (Tübingen: Mohr Siebeck, 2010); Hofreiter, *Making Sense of Old Testament Genocide*, 43–48.

27. Tertullian, *Against Heresies* 1.6.1. Quoted from http://newadvent.org/fathers/03121.htm.

28. Cowles, "Case for Radical Discontinuity," 41–43; Flood, *Disarming Scripture*, 75–89.

This approach of reevaluating the Old Testament also encounters a few other problems. First, the New Testament accepts the stories of the Old Testament, including the violent ones. For example, the destruction and judgment of Sodom is mentioned nine times in the New Testament, but is never condemned or explained as some kind of nonviolent action. Similarly, both Stephen and Paul refer to the conquest of Canaan without condemnation (Acts 7:45; 13:19). Second, this approach cannot draw a strong line between an angry and violent God in the Old Testament and a nonviolent God in the New Testament. One of the most commonly quoted verses in the Old Testament itself is Exodus 34:6: "The LORD, the LORD, a God merciful and gracious, slow to anger, and abounding in steadfast love and faithfulness." On the flip side, the New Testament also contains references to the wrath of God. Even after the resurrection of Jesus, divine violence does not cease, as may be seen in the striking of Elymas with blindness (Acts 13:11) and the deaths of Ananias, Sapphira, and Herod (Acts 5:1–11; 12:20–23).[29] Even Jesus himself is associated with violence, partly in the Gospels (with the cleansing of the temple in John 2:14–17 and the strong condemnations in Matt. 23), but especially in the book of Revelation.[30] Most dramatically, the eschatological judgment described throughout the New Testament appears to be quite violent.

---

29. One critique of Seibert says that his work "does not take seriously New Testament violence, the significance of ideological and/or structural violence, or the anti-Semitic implications of his own hermeneutics." Julia M. O'Brien, "Trauma All Around: Pedagogical Reflections on Victimization and Privilege in Theological Responses to Biblical Violence," in *La Violencia and the Hebrew Bible*, ed. Susanne Scholz and Pablo R. Andiñach, Semeia Studies 82 (Atlanta: SBL, 2016), 188.

30. Alan S. Bandy, "Vengeance, Wrath and Warfare as Images of Divine Justice in John's Apocalypse," in *Holy War in the Bible: Christian Morality and an Old Testament Problem*, ed. Heath A. Thomas, Jeremy Evans, and Paul Copan (Downers Grove, IL: InterVarsity Press, 2013), 108–29; Dana M. Harris, "Understanding Images of Violence in the Book of Revelation," in *Encountering Violence in the Bible*, ed. Markus Zehnder and Hallvard Hagelia, The Bible in the Modern World 55 (Sheffield: Sheffield Phoenix, 2013), 148–64.

Scholars who take this Christological approach respond to the violence in Revelation and eschatological judgment in a variety of ways. For the book of Revelation, they generally view it as symbolic based on the apocalyptic genre and therefore not as portraying actual violence.[31] Seibert attempts to differentiate between historical judgment and eschatological judgment based on whether or not it is inside of time: "If one accepts the conditionalists' [annihilationists'] view of eternal punishment, it is still possible to maintain that the God Jesus reveals acts nonviolently in historical time and is, therefore, fundamentally nonviolent even in the face of Jesus' teachings about eschatological judgment."[32] However, his claim that God's actions outside of historical time make no difference with respect to God's fundamental nature will strike many as special pleading: why would God be allowed to act against his character just because it is outside of time? John Dominic Crossan takes a more radical approach by rejecting eschatological judgment altogether: "The meaning of that Bible's story is in its middle, in the story of Jesus in the Gospels and the early writings of Paul; the climax of the narrative is in the center; and the sense of its nonviolent center judges the (non)sense of its violent ending."[33]

Summary

In sum, scholars who adhere to the second view of reevaluating the Old Testament tend to read the Old Testament narratives literally, believing that they contain depictions of genocide. However, for historical, ethical, or theological reasons they reject either entire texts or certain violent aspects of texts. Naturally, this has significant implications for the doctrine of inerrancy, as these scholars see either historical or ethical errors in the Old Testament. The subtitle of Thom

31. Seibert, *Disturbing Divine Behavior*, 254–57.
32. Seibert, *Disturbing Divine Behavior*, 253–54.
33. John Dominic Crossan, *How to Read the Bible and Still Be a Christian: Struggling with Divine Violence from Genesis to Revelation* (New York: Harper-One, 2015), 35.

Stark's book illustrates this: *The Human Faces of God: What Scripture Reveals When It Gets God Wrong (And Why Inerrancy Tries to Hide It)*. Wes Morriston's main point in bringing up the topic of genocide is the need to reject inerrancy.[34] If one wants to take this view and hold onto inerrancy, a different definition of inerrancy than has historically been accepted will be required.[35] Scholars in this group also tend to avoid doctrinal debates based on the Bible.[36] For example, Enns says that "the Bible is not a weapon, a sword to be wielded today against modern-day Canaanites or Babylonians. It is a book where we meet God."[37]

In spite of rejecting the violent texts, these scholars generally desire to retain the importance and relevance of the Old Testament. In general terms, John Collins recommends that the interpreter be less certain about proclaiming what the Bible teaches: "Perhaps the most constructive thing a biblical critic can do toward lessening the contribution of the Bible to violence in the world is to show that such certitude is an illusion."[38] Seibert calls for removing the corrosive aspects of a story while keeping the constructive parts. For example, in Exodus 15 readers should discard the image of God as a warrior, but keep God's hatred of injustice. In this way, readers do not reject these texts entirely, but only the offensive portions of them. Thus, believers can still learn even from these violent texts.[39] Thom Stark advocates keeping the rejected texts, but not as a guide to follow.

---

34. Wes Morriston, "Did God Command Genocide? A Challenge to the Biblical Inerrantist," *Philosophia Christi* 11 (2009): 7–26.

35. For example, Rauser defines his view as "functional inerrancy" (Randal Rauser, "Errant Statements in an Inerrant Book," 19 February 2013, http://randalrauser.com/2013/02/errant-statements-in-an-inerrant-book/, accessed December 31, 2020).

36. Flood, *Disarming Scripture*, 229–58.

37. Enns, *Bible Tells Me So*, 238.

38. Collins, *Does the Bible Justify Violence?*, 33.

39. Seibert, *Disturbing Divine Behavior*, 212–15; Eric A. Seibert, "Preaching from Violent Biblical Texts: Helpful Strategies for Addressing Violence in the Old Testament," *Perspectives in Religious Studies* 42 (2015): 247–57. For a similar view, see Sparks, *Sacred Word, Broken Word*, 111–12.

Instead, according to Stark, "They must be retained as scripture, precisely as condemned texts. Their status as condemned is exactly their scriptural value. That they are condemned is what they reveal to us about God."[40] That is, their rejection shows us that this is precisely how God does not act.

The reevaluation of the Old Testament provides obvious ethical benefits by disassociating God from biblical violence. However, it comes at the cost of being able to trust the Old Testament as a reliable document. Choosing this view also usually entails a rejection of inerrancy (or at least a significant redefinition of the idea). Since many Christians are uncomfortable with these views about the nature of God and the Bible, the social cost of taking this approach may be quite high—perhaps even leading to the loss of a job or removal from fellowship at a church.

40. Stark, *Human Faces of God*, 218.

Chapter Six

REEVALUATING THE INTERPRETATION
OF THE OLD TESTAMENT

Overview of View 3

A third group of scholars reevaluates the interpretation of these stories by arguing that the events in the Old Testament are not as violent as they appear. This group generally attempts to preserve the inspiration and inerrancy of the Old Testament, but is able to keep YHWH distant from the violence by declaring the violent texts to be nonviolent in some way (or at least minimally violent enough to be declared ethically permissible). In line with this viewpoint, these scholars argue that the events of the Old Testament should not be considered genocide. Paul Copan argues that God's commands in the Old Testament are not genocide because they are not based on racial hatred.[1] However, even if he is right about the lack of xenophobic attitudes, the definition of genocide noted in chapter two is not restricted to race, but also includes religion. In a later work, Copan and Matthew Flannagan appeal to the stricter legal definitions of genocide to deny that the actions of Joshua are genocide since they see the events as involving expulsion rather than extermination.[2] More generally,

1. Paul Copan, *Is God a Moral Monster? Making Sense of the Old Testament God* (Grand Rapids: Baker, 2011), 163–65. For a similar argument, see Wright, *God I Don't Understand*, 92; Preston Sprinkle, *Fight: A Christian Case for Non-Violence* (Colorado Springs: Cook, 2013), 77–78.
2. Paul Copan and Matthew Flannagan, *Did God Really Command Genocide? Coming to Terms with the Justice of God* (Grand Rapids: Baker, 2014), 125–30.

Eleonore Stump observes that the same actions can be appropriately described with different words. For example, is pain inflicted on your hand surgery or torture? It depends on the context. Even if the actions are exactly the same, the context might be sufficiently different to warrant using a different word than genocide.[3]

Spiritualization

One traditional way to reevaluate the interpretation of violent biblical narratives throughout church history was to spiritualize them, a practice some still follow today.[4] For example, John Cassian said that the seven Canaanite nations to be destroyed by the Israelites were seven vices that Christians are to defeat within themselves.[5] Augustine called for his listeners to break the idols in pagans' hearts, not in their homes.[6] Some Jewish readings understand the texts commanding the destruction of the Amalekites in similar terms: the Amalekites stand for anti-Semitism or the inner psychological desire for evil.[7] The problem with this view is that it does not really address the problem of dead Canaanites: spiritualization might be a way forward in the area of drawing significance from these texts for today, but it does not resolve the ethical question.[8] The only way for this solution to be

3. Eleonore Stump, "Reply to Morriston," in *Divine Evil? The Moral Character of the God of Abraham*, ed. Michael Bergmann, Michael J. Murray, and Michael C. Rea (Oxford: Oxford University Press, 2011), 204–7.

4. Richard Swinburne, "What Does the Old Testament Mean?," in Bergmann, Murray, and Rea, *Divine Evil? The Moral Character of the God of Abraham*, 209–25; Hofreiter, *Making Sense of Old Testament Genocide*, 57–108.

5. Joseph T. Lienhard, ed., *Exodus, Leviticus, Numbers, Deuteronomy*, Ancient Christian Commentary on Scripture (Downers Grove, IL: InterVarsity Press, 2001), 286.

6. Lienhard, *Exodus, Leviticus, Numbers, Deuteronomy*, 287.

7. Avi Sagi, "The Punishment of Amalek in Jewish Tradition: Coping with the Moral Problem," trans. Batya Stein, *HTR* 87 (1994): 330–36.

8. As John Collins says: "It is all very well to say that the Canaanites that we should root out are vice and sinfulness, but we still have texts that speak rather clearly of slaughtering human beings" (*Does the Bible Justify Violence?*, 29–30).

effective is if the historicity of the account is rejected, which would put the interpreter in the view discussed in the previous chapter. However, the church fathers appear to have accepted the destruction of the Canaanites as historical.[9]

Nonlethal Actions

Another argument in this view is to see the *herem* texts as nonlethal. Some scholars, such as R. W. L. Moberly and Nathan MacDonald, view the violent texts as metaphors. Moberly says that the *herem* command in Deuteronomy 7 is "a primary exposition of the implications of the *Shema*," an ancient Jewish prayer that begins with the command to love YHWH found in Deuteronomy 6:4–9.[10] In more detail, he explains his argument in this way:

> Whatever the "literal" interpretation of *ḥerem* in certain Old Testament narratives might appear to mean, and whether or not *ḥerem* was ever actually implemented in Israel's warfare, Deuteronomy 7, I suggest, presents *ḥerem* as a metaphor for religious fidelity which has only two primary practical expressions [prohibition of intermarriage and the destruction of the Canaanites' religious items], neither of which involve the taking of life.[11]

Such a reading of *herem* as a metaphor is encouraged by the close parallel to the Shema in 2 Kings 23:25, where Josiah has just demon-

---

9. Hofreiter, *Making Sense of Old Testament Genocide*, 60.

10. R. W. L. Moberly, "Toward an Interpretation of the Shema," in *Theological Exegesis: Essays in Honor of Brevard S. Childs*, ed. Christopher Seitz and Kathryn Greene-McCreight (Grand Rapids: Eerdmans, 1999), 134. See also R. W. L. Moberly, "Election and the Transformation of *Ḥērem*," in *The Call of Abraham: Essays on the Election of Israel in Honor of Jon D. Levenson*, ed. Gary A. Anderson and Joel S. Kaminsky, Christianity and Judaism in Antiquity 19 (Notre Dame: University of Notre Dame Press, 2013), 67–89; R. W. L. Moberly, *Old Testament Theology: Reading the Hebrew Bible as Christian Scripture* (Grand Rapids: Baker Academic, 2013), 53–71.

11. Moberly, "Toward an Interpretation of the Shema," 135.

strated his love for YHWH by destroying Canaanite religious items (though the word *herem* is not used there).[12] Further, the instructions in Deuteronomy 7 refer to Israel's actions when they are already in the land, not while they are entering the land during the conquest of Canaan (Deut. 7:1–2).[13] Naturally, the prohibition of intermarriage immediately after the *herem* command also encourages this metaphorical interpretation because a prohibition of intermarriage seems rather pointless if all of the Canaanites will be dead.[14] The speeches of Joshua at the end of his life (Josh. 23–24) in which he calls for separation from the Canaanites rather than their destruction illustrate this reading of *herem*, offering a commentary on Deuteronomy and Joshua.[15] In sum, instead of a command to slaughter humans, *herem* was a metaphor for the radical obedience God desires from his people.

One scholar who combines the two approaches of metaphor and spiritualization is Douglas Earl, who defends his metaphorical view of *herem* by following the reading practices of the early church.[16] He desires to read Joshua mythically, defining myth "as a particular cultural expression that testifies in an existentially engaging fashion to an imaginative world that seeks to shape the way in which the community and the individual lives, thinks and feels, especially as

12. Moberly, "Toward an Interpretation of the Shema," 136–37.

13. Nathan MacDonald, *Deuteronomy and the Meaning of "Monotheism,"* FAT 2:1 (Tübingen: Mohr Siebeck, 2003), 111.

14. MacDonald, *Deuteronomy and the Meaning of "Monotheism,"* 112.

15. Douglas Earl, "The Christian Significance of Deuteronomy 7," *JTI* 3 (2009): 44–45; Douglas Earl, *Reading Joshua as Christian Scripture*, JTISup 2 (Winona Lake, IN: Eisenbrauns, 2010), 109.

16. Earl, "Christian Significance of Deuteronomy 7"; Earl, *Reading Joshua as Christian Scripture*; Douglas Earl, *The Joshua Delusion? Rethinking Genocide in the Bible* (Eugene, OR: Cascade, 2010); Douglas Earl, "Holy War and חרם: A Biblical Theology of חרם," in *Holy War in the Bible: Christian Morality and an Old Testament Problem*, ed. Heath A. Thomas, Jeremy Evans, and Paul Copan (Downers Grove, IL: InterVarsity Press, 2013), 152–75. Likewise, Jerome Creach builds on the reading of Origen to argue that "the ban is indeed a metaphor for spiritual purity and devotion to God" (Jerome F. D. Creach, *Violence in Scripture*, Interpretation [Louisville: Westminster John Knox, 2013], 111).

these relate to God."[17] From this perspective, Earl states: "*Herem,* when associated with warfare or genocide, never seems to describe an actual practice of Israel in the present—*it is 'never now' in terms of its literal application. It only has a 'literal existence' in the world of the text, either of the past or the future but 'never now'.*"[18] It was strictly a symbol of separation in which the metaphorical meaning (separation) did not entail the "literal" meaning (killing Canaanites).[19]

The main problem with these approaches once again is that the narratives of Deuteronomy 1–3 and Joshua make it sound like the Israelites killed many Canaanites. MacDonald unequivocally states that the "slaughter of the Canaanites or anyone else is not envisaged" in *herem.*[20] However, in his discussion of following *herem* as an "obedience that may act against natural impulses" he cites as his prime example the destruction of the Amalekites in 1 Samuel 15. Saul showed that he did not love YHWH when he did not obey him; rather than killing the livestock and the king as YHWH commanded, Saul spared them.[21] MacDonald does not explain the apparent incongruity. Is this only a parable and not "real history"? Earl's combination of the two views entails the same problems when he argues that Joshua has nothing to do with holy war or conquest, but this creates an overly strict definition of warfare. The separation of the text from history is problematic for most scholars in this category, as is his use of the word "myth." While Earl carefully defines "myth," its ingrained popular usage as synonymous with "false" makes it a difficult word to use.[22] Similar to the previous argument, allegorizing the text leaves the problem of the original wording of the text: we still have dead

---

17. Earl, *Reading Joshua as Christian Scripture,* 47.

18. Earl, *Joshua Delusion?,* 60. Italics in original.

19. Earl, *Reading Joshua as Christian Scripture,* 94–112; Earl, "Holy War and חרם," 154–63.

20. MacDonald, *Deuteronomy and the Meaning of "Monotheism,"* 116.

21. MacDonald, *Deuteronomy and the Meaning of "Monotheism,"* 115.

22. Christopher J. H. Wright, "Response to Douglas Earl," in *The Joshua Delusion? Rethinking Genocide in the Bible,* by Douglas Earl (Eugene, OR: Cascade, 2010), 141–42.

Canaanites. One possible way to address these concerns is to view YHWH's commands as a metaphor that the Israelites misunderstood and took literally.

Although they do not employ the idea of metaphor, John Walton and J. Harvey Walton's view ends up in a similar place by defining *herem* as destroying identity rather than killing people: "Converting everyone is not the actual objective of the *herem* any more than killing everyone is; conversion would have accomplished it, but it is not expected (see Josh 11:20). . . . The objective is to remove the various Canaanite identities from the use of every individual who remains in the land, by one way or another."[23] Therefore, the command is not to kill Canaanites, but to remove their Canaanite identity. By this reasoning the saving of Rahab is not an exception to *herem* but an example of its outworking. The New Testament then picks up on this idea with its calls to put off our old self—our old identity—and put on our new self in Christ (e.g., Col. 3:1–17). However, although Walton and Walton say that killing Canaanites was rare, they contend that it still happened: "'Putting them to the sword' is an alternative to their normal expected fate, which was slavery. They are being killed not for the purpose of making them dead but to remove them from use as slaves."[24] Therefore, since we still have dead Canaanites, other lines of argument will need to be employed to solve the ethical problem.[25]

23. John H. Walton and J. Harvey Walton, *The Lost World of the Israelite Conquest: Covenant, Retribution, and the Fate of the Canaanites* (Downers Grove, IL: InterVarsity Press, 2017), 214.

24. Walton and Walton, *Lost World of the Israelite Conquest*, 173.

25. In addition, many evangelicals will disagree with Walton and Walton's views that the laws in the Old Testament, and even the principles behind them, are not a list of moral commands to follow: "The Bible as Scripture—that is, as the divinely inspired, authoritative word of God—does not provide us with moral knowledge because God's purpose in providing it for us does not include teaching us how to be moral" (Walton and Walton, *Lost World of the Israelite Conquest*, 98).

Hyperbole

A third approach in the view of reevaluating the interpretation of the Old Testament is to read the destruction of the Canaanites hyperbolically: the narratives employ a figure of speech that makes the actions sound worse than they are.[26] Based on this assumption, several scholars conclude that "the conquest of Canaan was far less widespread and harsh than many people assume."[27] The presence of hyperbole can be shown in three ways: linguistically, logically, and rhetorically.[28] *Linguistically*, universal terminology, such as "they devoted all in the city to destruction" (Josh. 6:21), tends to indicate hyperbole. *Logically*, it would be unlikely that they would literally kill every single person. As we will see in the next point, this idea of universal death conflicts with the use of the "banish" terminology used elsewhere. In addition, verbal similarity in descriptions of the destruction of Judah by the Babylonians—when the Israelites were not actually destroyed—indicates the presence of hyperbole.[29] As noted above, one text describes YHWH's action as sending Canaanites into exile, a phrase commonly used to describe YHWH's judgment of Israel (2 Kings 17:11). The contrast between "all the land" (Josh. 21:43) and "the land that yet remains" (Josh. 13:2) in the same book also

26. The difference between this approach and the previous approach is small. Whereas the previous approach focuses more on religious aspects and downplays the battle, this approach focuses more on the battle and how the language exaggerates the actual events of the battle.

27. Copan, *Is God a Moral Monster?*, 170–74. See also Nicholas Wolterstorff, "Reading Joshua," in Bergmann, Murray, and Rea, *Divine Evil? The Moral Character of the God of Abraham*, 243–56; Sprinkle, *Fight*, 80–87; Copan and Flannagan, *Did God Really Command Genocide?*; Joshua Ryan Butler, *The Skeletons in God's Closet: The Mercy of Hell, the Surprise of Judgment, the Hope of Holy War* (Nashville: Nelson, 2014), 228–31; Webb and Oeste, *Bloody, Brutal, and Barbaric*, 136–230.

28. Charles Cruise, "A Methodology for Detecting and Mitigating Hyperbole in Matthew 5:38–42," *JETS* 61 (2018): 83–104.

29. Webb and Oeste, *Bloody, Brutal, and Barbaric*, 167–69.

encourages us to read the book hyperbolically.[30] *Rhetorically*, these martial accounts parallel the ancient Near Eastern accounts that use hyperbole to demonstrate the power of the king and the god, as demonstrated in the work of K. Lawson Younger Jr.[31] In addition, the rhetoric of hyperbole might be present in references to the death of an entire population when in reality only the king and his soldiers were killed.[32]

Hyperbole certainly exists in Joshua (see Josh. 10:20 for a clear example[33]), but it is questionable whether it solves the ethical problem. Younger employs the argument that Israel wrote their warfare accounts in a way similar to other ancient nations as a way to defend the historicity of the book of Joshua. Since he bases his arguments for hyperbole on the similarity between Joshua and the texts of the ancient Near Eastern kingdoms, using hyperbole as a way to make the conquest more palatable would then transform kings like Ramses II and Ashurbanipal into much kinder figures as well. Since advocates of the hyperbole approach tend to view Old Testament violence as ethically better than ancient Near Eastern violence, this argument creates a catch-22 situation. For example, those who appeal to Younger to solve the Canaanite problem do not quote him when he declares:

> Israel's ideology is one of "terror." The destruction of the populations of enemy cities is a practice of an ideology of "calculated frightfulness." The execution and hanging of kings on trees must also be considered in the light of ancient Near Eastern ideologies of conquest. Such practices did "soften up" the opposition. The elimination of the population also enhances the speed of deculturation and hence colonization.[34]

---

30. Wolterstorff, "Reading Joshua," 252–55.

31. K. Lawson Younger Jr., *Ancient Conquest Accounts: A Study in Ancient Near Eastern and Biblical History Writing*, JSOTSup 98 (Sheffield: JSOT Press, 1990).

32. Webb and Oeste, *Bloody, Brutal, and Barbaric*, Appendix A.

33. However, for an argument against seeing even Joshua 10:20 as an example of hyperbole, see G. K. Beale, *The Morality of God in the Old Testament*, Christian Answers to Hard Questions (Phillipsburg, NJ: P&R, 2013), 33–42.

34. Younger, Jr., *Ancient Conquest Accounts*, 233–34.

The hyperbole argument necessitates further analysis of the historical reality behind the hyperbole: if the Israelites did not engage in a mass slaughter of Canaanite civilians, what actually happened? For those who propose hyperbole as an ethical defense of the violence against the Canaanites, two options are generally offered for the historical reality behind the hyperbole, which we will look at in the final two sections of this view.

Military Battle

One way forward is provided by Richard Hess, who argues that the killing in the book of Joshua was restricted to military battles, apart from civilians. While the accounts of the conquest of Jericho and Ai appear to involve the defeat of a settled city full of civilians, Hess shows how each part of this description could be interpreted in other ways.[35] For example, the word "city" can refer to a fort (2 Sam. 5:7; 12:26), while the walls might have been the exterior walls of a circle of houses around the city. The presence of Rahab at Jericho does not necessarily indicate the presence of other civilians; she and her family might have been the only noncombatants in the city. The phrase "men and women, young and old" in reference to those killed may simply be a stereotypical phrase meaning "all" and not a literal reference to civilians and children. The "king" could refer to a military leader or a commissioner.[36] In a similar vein, John Monson provides geographical evidence that the gate at Ai was actually a geographical feature, not a man-made architectural feature.[37]

---

35. This also solves the archaeological problem of the sites of both Jericho and Ai being empty at the purported time of conquest by Israel.

36. Richard S. Hess, "The Jericho and Ai of the Book of Joshua," in *Critical Issues in Early Israelite History*, ed. Richard S. Hess, Gerald A. Klingbeil, and Paul J. Ray, Jr., BBRSup 3 (Winona Lake, IN: Eisenbrauns, 2008), 33–46; Copan, *Is God a Moral Monster?*, 175–77.

37. John M. Monson, "Enter Joshua: The 'Mother of Current Debates' in Biblical Archaeology," in *Do Historical Matters Matter to Faith? A Critical Appraisal of Modern and Postmodern Approaches to Scripture*, ed. James K. Hoffmeier and Dennis R. Magary (Wheaton, IL: Crossway, 2012), 442–52.

The main problem with Hess's argument is that each part of his vision of the conquest is certainly possible, but his argument requires a large number of merely "possible" interpretations to come together to make it work. In addition, seeing Jericho as a military base would imply a stronger centralized government that had the power and wealth to support it. However, such a powerful government was not known to be present in the hill country during this time period. The Amarna letters portray many small city-states there fighting each other, not the kind of government that could afford to create and maintain a military outpost at the eastern foot of the highlands. Finally, most military camps throughout history have included civilians and families; only the most temporary bases—like those directly on the front lines—would have excluded civilians. If Jericho was a military base, it seems likely it would be a more permanent kind of encampment in which at least some civilians would have lived. Indeed, in a siege situation the civilians often fled to a fortified area for defense. Hess's argument would work better if the Israelites were fighting an army in the field rather than a fortified city.

Banishment

Another possible reality behind the hyperbole is banishment: the Canaanites were not killed, but forced to leave the land of Canaan.[38] Since, as noted earlier, the parallel texts about the Canaanites in Exodus, Leviticus, and Numbers imply banishment, some scholars conclude that the *herem* texts in Deuteronomy should be read in light of the earlier texts. Also as noted above, many other texts throughout the Old Testament describe the events of Joshua in terms of banish-

38. Copan, *Is God a Moral Monster?*, 181–82; David T. Lamb, *God Behaving Badly: Is the God of the Old Testament Angry, Sexist and Racist?* (Downers Grove, IL: InterVarsity Press, 2011), 100–101; Zehnder, " Annihilation of the Canaanites"; Copan and Flannagan, *Did God Really Command Genocide?*, 76–83; Butler, *Skeletons in God's Closet*, 232–33; L. Daniel Hawk, *The Violence of the Biblical God: Canonical Narrative and Christian Faith* (Grand Rapids: Eerdmans, 2019), 157; Webb and Oeste, *Bloody, Brutal, and Barbaric*, 231–62.

ment (Josh. 15:14; 24:18; Judg. 1:20; 6:9; 11:23; 1 Kings 14:24). Early Jewish tradition—such as the retelling of the events of Genesis in the book of Jubilees that dates to around 150 BCE—records that the land of Canaan belonged to Shem, but Canaan stole it.[39] Much later Jewish tradition portrays Joshua expelling the Canaanites—specifically the Girgashites—to their proper home in North Africa west of Egypt, where some Berber groups through medieval times claimed Canaanite descent.[40] The idea of defeated enemies abandoning their cities is also supported by the flight of Israelites from their cities at the defeat of Saul (1 Sam 31:7).

The problem with this view is twofold. First, as noted earlier, references to banishment appear less frequently in the text of Joshua than references to killing. Second, the banishment of an entire nation is still seriously ethically problematic, as exemplified by such cases as the relocation of the Armenians in Turkey during the First World War. In contemporary terms, this is called ethnic cleansing, a point that Copan and Flannagan freely admit.[41] While perhaps lessening the ethical problem, viewing the destruction of the Canaanites as banishment certainly does not solve it.

Summary

In sum, through a variety of means the scholars in this view reevaluate the interpretation of the Old Testament by arguing that the vio-

39. Katell Berthelot, "The Canaanites Who 'Trusted in God': An Original Interpretation of the Fate of the Canaanites in Rabbinic Literature," *JJS* 62 (2011): 233–61.

40. Paul Fenton, "The Canaanites in Africa: The Origins of the Berbers according to Medieval Muslim and Jewish Authors," in *The Gift of the Land and the Fate of the Canaanites in Jewish Thought*, ed. Katell Berthelot, Joseph E. David, and Marc Hirshman (Oxford: Oxford University Press, 2014), 297–310.

41. Copan and Flannagan, *Did God Really Command Genocide?*, 128–30, 326. Copan had earlier denied that this was ethnic cleansing because it was not based on racial hatred; see Paul Copan, "Yahweh Wars and the Canaanites: Divinely Mandated Genocide or Corporate Capital Punishment? Responses to Critics," *Philosophia Christi* 11 (2009): 76–77.

lent texts are not ethically problematic. While it might look like God has commanded horrible things, a close reading of the biblical text shows that this is not the case. This has immediate ethical benefits, asserting that YHWH did not command genocide, and it also keeps the Old Testament intact as a historical record. However, the social cost here is that many will see this position as playing fast and loose with the biblical text. Even if one is convinced that this reading of the text is correct, many will think that this interpretation is forcing the text into a predetermined mold to make it read in a predetermined fashion, especially when the benefits of this particular reading are so obvious.

Chapter Seven

REEVALUATING VIOLENCE IN
THE OLD TESTAMENT

Overview of View 4

Finally, the fourth group of scholars accepts the biblical stories as they are commonly understood (agreeing with the second view), but re-evaluate the ethics of the violence, arguing that YHWH was justified in his treatment of the Canaanites for a variety of reasons. Scholars in this view are not unified on whether we should use the word "genocide" to describe the events of Joshua. Several scholars argue that the term applies, mainly because the events in Joshua fulfill many of the criteria in the UN statement on genocide. Eugene Merrill delivers a clear opinion: "The issue, then, cannot be whether or not genocide is intrinsically good or evil—its sanction by a holy God settles that question."[1] However, scholars who combine this approach with arguments from view three (such as hyperbole and banishment) tend to reject the attribution of the term to the conquest.[2]

Mystery/Sovereignty

One argument often presented to defend the commanded violence is to appeal to mystery: God is sovereign and humans cannot under-

---

1. Eugene H. Merrill, "The Case for Moderate Continuity," in *Show Them No Mercy: Four Views on God and Canaanite Genocide* (Grand Rapids: Zondervan, 2003), 93.
2. Webb and Oeste, *Bloody, Brutal, and Barbaric*, 172.

stand his ways.[3] Howard Wettstein suggests that reading these texts puts us in a similar position to Job before the whirlwind, questioning what God is doing in the world but not receiving an answer.[4] This approach is often phrased as a call to read the violent texts in light of the entire canon so that we can have a fuller image of who God is: his violence must be held in tension with his mercy.[5] The social media phenomenon of creating a trailer for popular movies to portray them as if they are a different genre provides an example of what happens when people fixate on these violent texts at the expense of other texts; for example, one could portray *Mary Poppins* as a horror movie by selectively choosing certain scenes.[6] One variation of this approach is Stephen Williams's argument that God acted with a heavy heart, saddened at what had to be done.[7] Clearly, at some level Christians must appeal to divine sovereignty when discussing this question. However, while it might be the ultimate answer, an overly quick appeal to God's sovereignty can often inhibit further study or indicate a fear to think

3. Mark C. Murphy, "God Beyond Justice," in *Divine Evil? The Moral Character of the God of Abraham*, ed. Michael Bergmann, Michael J. Murray, and Michael C. Rea (Oxford: Oxford University Press, 2011), 150–67; Beale, *Morality of God in the Old Testament*, 12–16. Karl Barth also has an argument that fits into this category; see a summary in Hofreiter, *Making Sense of Old Testament Genocide*, 215–19.

4. Howard Wettstein, "God's Struggles," in Bergmann, Murray, and Rea, *Divine Evil? The Moral Character of the God of Abraham*, 332–33.

5. Christopher Seitz, "Canon and Conquest: The Character of the God of the Hebrew Bible," in Bergmann, Murray, and Rea, *Divine Evil? The Moral Character of the God of Abraham*, 292–308; Kirsten Nielson, "The Violent God of the Old Testament: Reading Strategies and Responsibility," in *Encountering Violence in the Bible*, ed. Markus Zehnder and Hallvard Hagelia, The Bible in the Modern World 55 (Sheffield: Sheffield Phoenix, 2013), 207–15.

6. Dan Kimball, *How (Not) to Read the Bible: Making Sense of the Anti-Women, Anti-Science, Pro-Violence, Pro-Slavery and Other Crazy-Sounding Parts of Scripture* (Grand Rapids: Zondervan, 2020), 271–72.

7. Stephen N. Williams, "Could God Have Commanded the Slaughter of the Canaanites?," *TynBul* 63 (2012): 161–78. For a similar thought, see Jeph Holloway, "The Ethical Dilemma of Holy War," *Southwestern Journal of Theology* 41 (1998): 62.

deeply about the topic. In addition, this defense feels lacking to many. As Enns states, *"Is this really the kind of God we believe in, the God who created the world and loves it?"*[8]

Wickedness of the Canaanites

One of the most common arguments for the justness of the violence against the Canaanites is that the Canaanites were wicked, as shown through both biblical texts (Gen. 15:16; Lev. 18:25; Deut. 9:4–5; 2 Chron. 28:3) and Ugaritic myths. This reasoning goes back to ancient times, as demonstrated in chapter 12 of the apocryphal book Wisdom of Solomon (called a deuterocanonical book in the Roman Catholic tradition) and in the writings of Philo.[9] The Canaanites are portrayed as sexually immoral, idolatrous, and bloodthirsty (although this last accusation could be viewed ironically in light of the command to destroy them). Because they act in these ways, then their punishment was deserved.[10] The New Testament suggests that the Canaanites knew how YHWH wanted them to act and rejected his commands (Heb. 11:31). In the bigger picture, idolatry is a serious affair and reflects cosmic realities. The situation is not comparable to a stronger nation invading a weaker nation, but a police force invading a Mafia hideout to restore order and establish justice.[11] However, most of these scholars do not argue that Canaan was worse than

---

8. Enns, *Bible Tells Me So*, 41. Italics in original.

9. Arie Versluis, "The Early Reception History of the Command to Exterminate the Canaanites," *Biblical Reception* 3 (2014): 310, 319–20.

10. Wright, *God I Don't Understand*, 92–93; Clay Jones, "We Don't Hate Sin So We Don't Understand What Happened to the Canaanites: An Addendum to 'Divine Genocide' Arguments," *Philosophia Christi* 11 (2009): 53–72; Copan, *Is God a Moral Monster?*, 59–61; Lamb, *God Behaving Badly*, 78–80; Sprinkle, *Fight*, 76; Copan and Flannagan, *Did God Really Command Genocide?*, 66–68; Butler, *Skeletons in God's Closet*, 233–40; Arie Versluis, *The Command to Exterminate the Canaanites: Deuteronomy 7*, OtSt 71 (Leiden: Brill, 2017), 354–57.

11. Copan, *Is God a Moral Monster?*, 167–68. See also Merrill, "Case for Moderate Continuity," 81–84.

other nations.[12] In general, they emphasize the importance of divine anger and judgment as the means of bringing peace and order to the world.[13] The destruction of the Canaanites has also been connected to the curse of Canaan, especially in Jewish circles.[14] Finally, as described in chapter three, Heiser argues that the eradication of the sinful Nephilim was the goal of the conquest of Canaan.

However, this argument is not as straightforward as it might appear when quoting the relevant biblical texts. The book of Joshua does not refer at all to the wickedness of the Canaanites. Even if we do grant their depravity, we are still left with the problem of the restricted nature of the conquest. Why were only the Canaanites condemned? Were they worse sinners than other nations? It seems that this would be a very hard argument to make, especially when texts like Leviticus 18:3 combine the wickedness of Canaan with that of Egypt. In addition, William Webb and Gordon Oeste point out that just because the Canaanites were guilty does not mean that they were then liable to any kind of punishment: their massacre as a people would still be an unjust punishment.[15] The Canaanites' depravity has also been questioned. For example, Richard Hess argues that the West Semitic wisdom tradition illustrates that the Canaanites were not uniformly wicked.[16]

12. See the quotation from Copan: "I'm not arguing that the Canaanites were the worst specimens of humanity that ever existed, nor I am arguing that the Canaanites won the immorality contest for worst-behaved peoples in the ancient Near East" (Copan, *Is God a Moral Monster?*, 160).

13. Melvin Tinker, *Mass Destruction: Is God Guilty of Genocide?* (Welwyn Garden City, UK: Evangelical Press, 2017), 71–92.

14. Menahem Kister, "The Fate of the Canaanites and the Despoliation of the Egyptians: Polemics among Jews, Pagans, Christians, and Gnostics: Motifs and Motives," in *The Gift of the Land and the Fate of the Canaanites in Jewish Thought*, ed. Katell Berthelot, Joseph E. David, and Marc Hirshman (Oxford: Oxford University Press, 2014), 68–74; Versluis, *Command to Exterminate the Canaanites*, 361.

15. Webb and Oeste, *Bloody, Brutal, and Barbaric*, 41–45.

16. Richard S. Hess, "'Because of the Wickedness of These Nations' (Deut 9:4–5): The Canaanites—Ethical or Not?," in *For Our Good Always: Studies on the Message and Influence of Deuteronomy in Honor of Daniel I. Block*, ed. Jason S. DeRouchie, Jason Gile, and Kenneth J. Turner (Winona Lake, IN: Eisenbrauns, 2013), 17–38. For a response to his argument, see Hélène M. Dallaire, "Taking

From a different direction, John Walton and Harvey Walton argue strenuously against the connection between the wickedness of the Canaanites and YHWH's judgment because they are not under a covenant with God.[17] They contend that "none of the normal Hebrew words indicating crime and punishment are ever used to describe the Canaanites or their actions. The descriptions of Canaanite nations in Leviticus 18 and Deuteronomy 9 are, in context, invoking a well-established ancient Near Eastern literary trope about hordes of invincible barbarians who are established by the gods to cause trouble for the servants of the gods before being destroyed by the gods."[18]

Uniqueness of the Land of Canaan

Rather than their exceptional sin, some connect the reason for the commanded destruction of the Canaanites to the land of Canaan: the Canaanites are targets only because they are in the land promised to Israel.[19] As noted in chapter six, early Jewish tradition records that the land of Canaan belonged to Shem, but Canaan stole it. More broadly, since Israel has to be protected from idolatry, Canaanite religion needs to be removed from the land.[20] Therefore, the Canaanites are free to stay if they renounce their religion, but otherwise the land of Canaan must be free from Canaanites. L. Daniel Hawk notes that the texts judging Canaanite sin are found in contexts emphasizing the land

---

the Land by Force: Divine Violence in Joshua," in *Wrestling with the Violence of God: Soundings in the Old Testament*, ed. M. Daniel Carroll R. and J. Blair Wilgus, BBRSup 10 (Winona Lake, IN: Eisenbrauns, 2015), 69–71.

17. Walton and Walton, *Lost World of the Israelite Conquest*, 75–166.

18. Walton and Walton, *Lost World of the Israelite Conquest*, 256.

19. Copan and Flannagan, *Did God Really Command Genocide?*, 62–66. See also the argument of Nahmanides in Joseph E. David, "Nahmanides on Law, Land, and Otherness," in *The Gift of the Land and the Fate of the Canaanites in Jewish Thought*, ed. Katell Berthelot, Joseph E. David, and Marc Hirshman (Oxford: Oxford University Press, 2014), 180–201.

20. Merrill, "Case for Moderate Continuity," 86–87; Holloway, "Ethical Dilemma of Holy War," 56–57; Copan and Flannagan, *Did God Really Command Genocide?*, 68–70.

promise.[21] One variation of this argument is to see the land of Canaan as sacred space that would permit only the worship of YHWH.[22] While this argument helps to show why the massacre commands are not to be used as a warrant for contemporary wars, it will not help most readers with the ethical problem of the destruction of the Canaanites.

On a related note, Eleonore Stump speculates that the commanded destruction of the Amalekites was designed to show what would not work "to cure them [the Israelites] of what needs to be healed in them." In other words, the removal of the sinful Canaanites was not going to solve the Israelites' sin problem: another solution was needed. Even a purified land of Canaan would not be sufficient for Israel to avoid breaking covenant with YHWH.[23] While such a reading is possible, it is not mentioned in the text and requires a backward reading from the New Testament.

God's Judgment of Sin Regardless of Ethnicity

Another common argument to defend God's violent actions is that they are based on people's relationship with him, not ethnicity.[24] On the one hand, God is more gracious to the Canaanites than it first

21. Hawk, *Violence of the Biblical God*, 144–45.

22. Webb and Oeste, *Bloody, Brutal, and Barbaric*, 249–61. In an article dealing with the reason for the expulsion of the Canaanites rather than the means of expulsion, Gary A. Anderson argues that "in the Bible's understanding, the land that Israel will inhabit has a certain sanctity that makes it different from all the other lands of the earth. It cannot bear oppressive or licentious behavior (see Lev. 18:24–30). God, due to his abundant mercy, will be patient with such activity up to a point. In Abraham's day, the Canaanites were granted some four hundred years to amend their ways; the Israelites would, in turn, be granted a similar amount of time prior to their exile at the hand of the Babylonians" (Gary A. Anderson, "What about the Canaanites?," in Bergmann, Murray, and Rea, *Divine Evil? The Moral Character of the God of Abraham*, 282).

23. See Eleonore Stump, "The Problem of Evil and the History of Peoples: Think Amalek," in Bergmann, Murray, and Rea, *Divine Evil? The Moral Character of the God of Abraham*, 194.

24. Copan, *Is God a Moral Monster?*, 163–65; Copan and Flannagan, *Did God Really Command Genocide?*, 70–74.

appears. The Canaanites are given time and opportunity to repent. Their judgment is announced in Genesis 15:16, many centuries before the Israelites conquer Canaan.[25] The clearest example of Canaanite repentance is Rahab, who confesses the power of YHWH and becomes a part of Israel.[26] It is also possible that going around the city of Jericho multiple times is intended as an opportunity for them to turn to follow YHWH.[27] Although no specific examples are recorded in the biblical text, according to early Jewish writings Joshua sent messengers of peace to the Canaanite cities before they were conquered. Jewish tradition notes that although YHWH orders Moses to fight Sihon without any reference to seeking peace first, Moses's first action is to send messengers of peace to Sihon (Deut. 2:24–26).[28] This pattern shows us that the Israelites should still have sent messengers of peace in spite of YHWH's command to destroy the Canaanites. Wisdom of Solomon 12:10 also attributes the slow progress of the conquest to the need to give the Canaanites time to repent. The prophetic literature records that God intended to redeem the Canaanites (Zech. 9:7).[29]

---

25. Lamb, *God Behaving Badly*, 39–41; Anderson, "What about the Canaanites?," 280.

26. Daniel I. Block, *Deuteronomy*, NIVAC (Grand Rapids: Zondervan, 2012), 485. See also William A. Ford, "What about the Gibeonites?," *TynBul* 66 (2015): 197–216. In another paper Ford suggests that we view the Canaanites as a challenge for Israel in both a positive and a negative sense: positive in the sense of following the example of the godly Canaanites and negative in the sense of a warning about what would happen to Israel if they acted like Canaan (William A. Ford, "The Challenge of the Canaanites," *TynBul* 68 [2017]: 161–84).

27. Richard S. Hess, *Joshua: An Introduction and Commentary*, Tyndale Old Testament Commentaries (Downers Grove, IL: InterVarsity Press, 1996), 142–43; Copan, *Is God a Moral Monster?*, 178; Sprinkle, *Fight*, 79.

28. For a brief survey of this position in Jewish literature (though they both reject it), see Jeffrey H. Tigay, *Deuteronomy*, The JPS Torah Commentary (Philadelphia: Jewish Publication Society, 1996), 472, 539; Moshe Weinfeld, "The Ban on the Canaanites in the Biblical Codes and Its Historical Development," in *History and Traditions of Early Israel: Studies Presented to Eduard Nelson, May 8th, 1993*, ed. André Lemaire and Benedikt Otzen, VTSup 50 (Leiden: Brill, 1993), 154–55.

29. Copan, *Is God a Moral Monster?*, 187–88; Wright, *God I Don't Understand*, 99–106.

The archaeological continuity between the Canaanite and Israelite settlements in the highlands might also support the idea that many Canaanites decided to join the Israelites. Lawson Stone suggests that the call to cast off idols in Joshua 24 would have been directed primarily at these Canaanites who joined Israel.[30] Richard Swinburne even says that the destruction of the Canaanites provided a good opportunity for them:

> For example, of course God loves the Canaanites; but it is good for them, as for all of us, to have the opportunity of forming our characters by means of heroic choices—which only become available to us in the face of suffering and death. And I re-emphasize that God does not wrong the Canaanites (including their children) if he makes the gift of life shorter for some of them than for some other humans. If there is a God, he has made it abundantly clear that the "gift" of life is a temporary one which he makes as long or short as he chooses.[31]

On the other hand, YHWH also judges Israel when they sin. If Israel were to act like the Canaanites, YHWH would judge them in the same way he judged the Canaanites (Lev. 18:28; Deut. 28:25–68).[32] When the Israelites become worse than the Canaanites at the end of the book of Judges, as illustrated in the comparison of the Israelite city Gibeah to Sodom and Gomorrah (compare Judg. 19 with Gen. 19), then *herem* is effectively brought against the tribe of Benjamin (Judg. 20). God is not racist, but judges all those who oppose him and act in sinful ways. His primary opponent is sin, not the Canaanites.

However, the problem with this view is that it does not really solve the problem of God and violence, but only makes it worse: he not

---

30. Lawson G. Stone, "Early Israel and Its Appearance in Canaan," in *Ancient Israel's History: An Introduction to Issues and Sources*, ed. Bill T. Arnold and Richard S. Hess (Grand Rapids: Baker Academic, 2014), 155–56.

31. Richard Swinburne, "Reply to Morriston," in Bergmann, Murray, and Rea, *Divine Evil? The Moral Character of the God of Abraham*, 233.

32. Wright, *God I Don't Understand*, 95–96; Webb and Oeste, *Bloody, Brutal, and Barbaric*, Appendix C.

only violently attacks other nations but also his own people.[33] The idea that Israel engaged in missionary activity before they killed the Canaanites is comforting, but the book of Joshua provides little evidence that this happened. Further, what would have happened if the Canaanites repented? Would Israel still have received the land? What would have happened to the Abrahamic promise?[34]

Redemptive Trajectory

William Webb has proposed a redemptive trajectory hermeneutic as a way forward for reading a variety of biblical texts, most prominently in regard to corporal punishment, slavery, and the role of women. His hermeneutic emphasizes how God meets his people in their current cultural location but also calls them to a higher ethic. In a book co-authored with Gordon Oeste Webb has now fleshed out his trajectory hermeneutic in the area of warfare in the Old Testament.[35] They spend a large part of their book arguing for a hyperbolic and banishment understanding of the warfare texts, as summarized in the previous chapter. However, they do not see these arguments as solving the ethical problem, which places them in this fourth view. They argue that rather than calling the Israelites to the ideal good that would have been impossible for Israel to do in their cultural context, God accommodated himself to the Old Testament Israelites by showing ways they could begin an upward ethical trajectory toward the ideal and away from the atrocities of the ancient Near East. However, as part of that accommodation some injustices were left embedded in Israelite life. For example, they see the war bride law (Deut. 21:10–14) as a law that is still morally problematic but also offers an advance over ancient Near Eastern cultures that had no parallel law and practiced battlefield rape.[36] While the

33. Stark, *Human Faces of God*, 114–15.

34. Nicholas Wolterstorff, "Comments on 'What about the Canaanites?'" in Bergmann, Murray, and Rea, *Divine Evil? The Moral Character of the God of Abraham*, 287.

35. Webb and Oeste, *Bloody, Brutal, and Barbaric*.

36. Webb and Oeste, *Bloody, Brutal, and Barbaric*, 84–127.

law is certainly not the ethical ideal and perpetuates injustice against the captive woman, it lessens that injustice compared to how she would have been treated by other ancient Near Eastern cultures.

This trajectory is seen already in the Old Testament with texts that portray an "uneasy war God," such as in creation without conflict, the prohibition against killing prisoners (2 Kings 6:8–23), and YHWH's refusal to allow David to build the temple because of the blood on his hands (1 Chron. 22:6–10; 28:3).[37] This upward trajectory continues with Jesus, who rejects all kinds of violence, and culminates in a nonviolent eschatology that "unfolds a vision of God's unaccommodated ethical actions finally bringing the enactment of justice without embedded injustices; Jesus as the apocalyptic warrior transforms Old Testament war traditions."[38]

One problem with this view is that the word *herem* and events that look like genocide are relatively rare in the ancient Near East. As noted earlier, a few texts record kings proclaiming that they killed everyone in a conquered city, but overall *herem*-type destruction is uncommon. Rather than accommodating himself to the cultural surroundings in which he meets the Israelites in their ethical ignorance but begins the process of elevating them beyond their cultural context, YHWH appears to have gone beyond the standard warfare patterns in intensity. Another problem is the redemptive hermeneutic itself, as many evangelicals have rejected it with respect to other topics and most likely would here as well.[39] For example, many will undoubtedly be nervous about the level of critique Webb and Oeste lodge against violent texts in the Old Testament that are associated with YHWH. Finally, some might question why God accommodated himself to Israel rather than teaching

---

37. Webb and Oeste, *Bloody, Brutal, and Barbaric*, 288–316.

38. Webb and Oeste, *Bloody, Brutal, and Barbaric*, 354.

39. For example, see the responses to Webb's proposal in Gary T. Meadors, ed., *Four Views on Moving Beyond the Bible to Theology* (Grand Rapids: Zondervan, 2009).

them better patterns of life, especially when it comes to something so harmful as genocide.[40]

Parallel with Flood and Exodus

Another argument to defend God's violence against the Canaanites is to appeal to the parallels in the flood and the exodus.[41] Fewer Christians have problems with the ethics of the flood, but the parallel between the flood and God's violence against the Canaanites is quite striking: God destroys a very large number of people from all stages of life. L. Daniel Hawk emphasizes the anti-creation theme of the flood: "Yahweh accelerates the inevitable death-spiral of creation and saves a righteous man and his family, along with pairs of every species of creature, with the intention of beginning anew once the world reverts back to chaos."[42] In a related argument, Hawk sees the Canaanite conquest as parallel to the exodus, as they both "constitute the beginning and end of a creative work in which Yahweh brings a new people into being through deliverance, covenant, and inheritance."[43]

Of course, many who condemn the Canaanite destruction would also reject the flood. In addition, the flood and the violence against the Canaanites are not exactly the same. The main difference between the two is that the punishment is executed by Israelite soldiers under YHWH's control rather than the water under YHWH's control. Presumably, this would have been a traumatic time for the Israelite soldiers, leading to many cases of PTSD and other trauma. Would God really have ordered his people to undergo such traumatic actions?[44] These scholars respond that warfare was a more natural part of life

40. For their response to this critique, see Webb and Oeste, *Bloody, Brutal, and Barbaric*, Appendix E.

41. Walter C. Kaiser, Jr., *Toward Old Testament Ethics* (Grand Rapids: Zondervan, 1983), 268–69.

42. Hawk, *Violence of the Biblical God*, 44.

43. Hawk, *Violence of the Biblical God*, 151.

44. Rauser, "'Let Nothing That Breathes Remain Alive,'" 35–37.

in ancient times. Just because we find something traumatic does not necessarily make it evil. For those who live in a sanitized suburbia and buy meat neatly packaged in supermarkets, just seeing the sacrifices performed in the temple would have been traumatic.[45] Hawk also argues that the difference in human involvement between the exodus and the destruction of the Canaanites is only a matter of scope.[46]

Parallel with Eschatological Judgment

Similar to the previous point, some defend the Canaanite destruction by comparing it with the final judgment.[47] Meredith Kline argues that the conquest was an example of "intrusion ethics," in which the normal pattern of life in the eschaton (the end times) intrudes into the present arena of history and disturbs the common grace that is generally given to all.[48] From this perspective, the only unusual aspect of these events is the timing, as they are a foreshadowing of the final judgment, which all humans deserve. As we read the stories in Joshua, Phillip Cary argues we should read from the perspective of the Canaanites, reminding ourselves that this is the same fate we deserve.[49] Arie Versluis shows how the Canaanites become a symbol of evil elsewhere in the Old Testament, giving the conquest an eschatological tone.[50] This eschatological reading is supported by the eschatological

45. Copan, *Is God a Moral Monster?*, 189–91.

46. Hawk, *Violence of the Biblical God*, 151.

47. Daniel I. Block, "How Can We Bless You? Wrestling with Divine Violence in Deuteronomy," in *Wrestling with the Violence of God: Soundings in the Old Testament*, ed. M. Daniel Carroll R. and J. Blair Wilgus, BBRSup 10 (Winona Lake, IN: Eisenbrauns, 2015), 46–47; Beale, *Morality of God in the Old Testament*, 17–30.

48. Meredith G. Kline, "The Intrusion and the Decalogue," *WTJ* 16 (1953): 1–22; Daniel L. Gard, "The Case for Eschatological Continuity," in *Show Them No Mercy: Four Views on God and Canaanite Genocide* (Grand Rapids: Zondervan, 2003), 129–41. See also Tremper Longman, "The Case for Spiritual Continuity," in *Show Them No Mercy: Four Views on God and Canaanite Genocide* (Grand Rapids: Zondervan, 2003), 183–87.

49. Phillip Cary, "We Are All Rahab Now," *Christianity Today*, July/August 2013, 26–29.

50. Versluis, *Command to Exterminate the Canaanites*, 358–62.

associations commonly made with the land of Canaan, which became a symbol of heaven (for example, see Heb. 3–4; Rev. 21–22). If the conquest has positive eschatological connections, then it would not be surprising to see eschatological connections with judgment as well. While the New Testament does not connect the conquest with judgment, it does employ Sodom in this way; for example, 2 Peter 2:6 states that Sodom was an example of what would happen to the ungodly. These references encourage a similar reading of the conquest as a foreshadowing of eschatological judgment.

However, an eschatological view suffers various problems as well. Those who reject eschatological judgment altogether will not find this view helpful.[51] It also requires a canonical reading of the Bible as a whole, as reading the Old Testament—which has very few references to personal eschatology at all—on its own would most likely not allow one to reach this view. Finally, even if the parallels to eschatology are granted, the specifics of war in the Old Testament could still be critiqued. For example, the conquests of Israel by Assyria and Babylon also foreshadow eschatological judgment, but God judges these nations for how they completed their conquest of Israel.[52]

The Death of Children

The most troubling aspect of the killing of the Canaanites is the death of the children. How could one possibly rationalize the slaughter of a large number of innocent babies? Rauser calls this the NEBB belief: "never ever bludgeon babies," which most people hold as a very basic belief.[53] Many of the scholars in both the reevaluating the interpretation of the Old Testament view and the reevaluating violence in the Old Testament view deny that any children actually died, so they

---

51. Stephen N. Williams, "Theological Horizons of Joshua," in *Joshua*, ed. J. Gordon McConville and Stephen N. Williams, Two Horizons (Grand Rapids: Eerdmans, 2010), 123. For the argument that Jesus's words about hell refer to the conquest of Jerusalem in 70 CE by the Romans, see Enns, *Bible Tells Me So*, 42–43.

52. Webb and Oeste, *Bloody, Brutal, and Barbaric*, 45–50.

53. Rauser, "'Let Nothing That Breathes Remain Alive,'" 33–35.

do not address the topic. For example, those who read the texts as hyperbole would say that the only dead Canaanites were adults.

For those scholars who think that children were killed, they offer a variety of ethical defenses. One possible reply is to say that the children would have gone straight into the presence of God, based on ideas about the age of accountability.[54] This is possible, but the concept of the age of accountability is far from a certain biblical doctrine, and it is unclear how much the Israelites of Joshua's time would have known about personal eschatology. This argument also has problems due to modern cases of parents killing their children to ensure that they go directly to heaven. Why would we condemn this but not the killing of the Canaanite children?

Another response involves the idea of corporate solidarity, in which groups experience blessings and curses together as a community rather than as distinct individuals.[55] Many ancient cultures, as well as many cultures today, place more emphasis on community than on the individual.[56] Because the Canaanites as a whole had rejected YHWH and acted sinfully, then the punishment comes upon them as a whole.[57] Naturally, many people in the more individualistic Western world will not find such ideas satisfying.

Summary

In sum, scholars who belong in the fourth view deal with the problem of divine violence by reevaluating the ethics of violence for this one particular historical moment. The claims of biblical authority and proper hermeneutics overrule the claims of an innate human ethic,

54. Copan, *Is God a Moral Monster?*, 189.

55. Block, *Deuteronomy*, 485; Holloway, "Ethical Dilemma of Holy War," 61–62; Versluis, *Command to Exterminate the Canaanites*, 357–58.

56. E. Randolph Richards and Richard James, *Misreading Scripture with Individualist Eyes: Patronage, Honor, and Shame in the Biblical World* (Downers Grove, IL: IVP Academic, 2020).

57. For more on corporate solidarity in Israel, see Joel S. Kaminsky, *Corporate Responsibility in the Hebrew Bible*, JSOTSup 196 (Sheffield: Sheffield Academic, 1995).

and they are left with the difficult task of defending God's role in what looks suspiciously like genocide.

Obviously, the main problem with this argument is that it associates YHWH with violence, which will be appalling to many.[58] Additionally, this position leaves open the possibility of using the events in Joshua as a justification for modern genocide. Of course, arguments can be made to state why it was permissible in the Old Testament but is not today. For example, Daniel Heimbach differentiates between a crusading ethic and a just war ethic, arguing that the former is only valid under three conditions: (1) it is initiated specifically and only by God, (2) it is led only by God, and (3) it is "initiated and led by God *in a manner that could be verified* by those called to participate."[59] However, these criteria still allow for the possibility that God could call his people to do something similar today. This is not an implausible problem, as some in church history have claimed Joshua as precedent for their own violent actions (though none would qualify as a crusading ethic under Heimbach's categories).[60] For example, Alfred Cave details how many colonists did exactly this to Native Americans:[61]

---

58. As Gerd Lüdemann says, "At no time can there be different opinions on genocide" (Gerd Lüdemann, *The Unholy in Holy Scripture: The Dark Side of the Bible*, trans. John Bowden [Louisville: Westminster John Knox, 1997], 54).

59. Daniel R. Heimbach, "Crusade in the Old Testament and Today," in *Holy War in the Bible: Christian Morality and an Old Testament Problem*, ed. Heath A. Thomas, Jeremy Evans, and Paul Copan (Downers Grove, IL: InterVarsity Press, 2013), 196. Italics in original. For a similar argument, see Matthew Rowley, "The Epistemology of Sacralized Violence in the Exodus and Conquest," *JETS* 57 (2014): 63–84; Copan and Flannagan, *Did God Really Command Genocide?*, 233–56.

60. For a summary of this evidence, see Hofreiter, *Making Sense of Old Testament Genocide*, 160–213; Jenkins, *Laying Down the Sword*, 99–141. In the Israeli-Palestinian conflict, some Jewish settlers have talked about the Palestinians in terms of the Canaanites. See Nur Masalha, "Reading the Bible with the Eyes of the Canaanites: Neo-Zionism, Political Theology and the Land Traditions of the Bible (1967 to Gaza 2009)," *Holy Land Studies* 8 (2009): 58–59.

61. Alfred A. Cave, "Canaanites in a Promised Land: The American Indian and the Providential Theory of Empire," *American Indian Quarterly* 12 (1988): 277–97. See

When Americans were colonizing North America, Robert Gray declared that the English, like the Old Testament Israelites, had become a "great people" unnaturally confined in a "narrow land." God, recognizing both England's greatness and her economic need for more territory, had offered her Virginia as the English Canaan. Countering the possible objection that North America properly belonged to the Indians, Gray declared that while God "had given the earth to the children of men," the native Virginians could not rightfully share in that gift, as they partook of "the nature of beasts." Indeed, given "their godless ignorance and blasphemous idolatry," Gray held that the Indians were "worse than those beasts which are of most wild and savage nature."[62]

This fourth category has the benefit of a high view of Scripture and a straightforward hermeneutic. Nevertheless, the cost here is high as well: it associates YHWH with something that looks a lot like genocide. Even if one thinks that they can defend this and live with such a belief, the social cost will be that many others will be repulsed by such a god and might also question the sanity and compassion of one who follows such a god.[63] In addition, this belief could make evangelism more difficult.

also Robert Allen Warrior, "Canaanites, Cowboys, and Indians: Deliverance, Conquest, and Liberation Theology Today," *Christianity and Crisis* 49 (1989): 261–66.

62. Cave, "Canaanites in a Promised Land," 283.

63. For example, see Richard Dawkins's refusal to debate William Lane Craig because of this issue in http://www.theguardian.com/commentisfree/2011/oct/20/richard-dawkins-william-lane-craig. Accessed July 30, 2020.

CONCLUSION

I expect that many of you are in a place where, even though you now have more knowledge about the problem, you do not necessarily know which answer you will go with. Indeed, you might even feel worse about the problem now than when you began this book! I believe that this position is permissible: we are not required to land on a particular position for the sake of our faith. I find a comparison with the story in John 6 helpful in this regard. Jesus's statement that "unless you eat the flesh of the Son of Man and drink his blood, you have no life in you" (John 6:53) is not received well by the crowd, and many people leave him. At this point, Jesus asks his disciples if they are also going to leave. Peter responds, "Lord, to whom shall we go? You have the words of eternal life" (John 6:66–68). While Peter does not directly say this, the subtext of this statement seems to be that the disciples are as displeased with Jesus's statement as the crowd. However, in contrast to the crowd, their faith in Jesus might be shaken but not broken. In the grand scheme of their belief, they realize that as troubling as these latest statements by Jesus are, he has the words of life that no one else does.

In his discussion of moral injury potentially caused by Scripture, Brad Kelle refers to lament as a helpful way forward.[1] The laments in the book of Psalms provide a way for people to bring their problems to God and even rebuke him for his role in their struggles. For example, Psalm 13 begins in this way: "How long, O LORD? Will you forget me

1. Kelle, *Bible and Moral Injury*, 165–66.

forever? How long will you hide your face from me?" (Ps. 13:1). However, the laments then guide the Israelites in their grief back to a place of trust in YHWH. This process does not usually happen through a change in circumstance in which their lives outwardly improve, but through other means, such as prayer (Ps. 13:3–4), a change in perspective (Ps. 73:16–28), remembering God's faithfulness in the past (Ps 77:10–20), speaking theological truth to yourself (Ps. 42:5–6), and meditating on the word of God (Ps. 1). These laments can provide a pathway for us as we approach difficult texts in the Old Testament. They invite us to speak to God about our grievances in regard to these texts, but not necessarily expect God to fix our problem immediately by providing us with the "magic solution." Instead, like the laments, we should expect a process of restoring our trust in God. This happens best in community: the communal nature of many of the laments in the Psalms encourages believers to lament together too.

As a Christian, though I can certainly understand such a move, I emphatically reject the first approach that discards God and the Bible altogether. However, as I noted at the beginning of the book, my goal is not to convince you of the "correct solution" to the problem of the destruction of the Canaanites among the other three options. Instead, I hope that I have inspired you to think more deeply about the problem and that you have a better understanding of the various solutions. As you continue to wrestle with this issue in the context of your Christian community, may you continue to follow the one who has "the words of life" (John 6:68).

BIBLIOGRAPHY

Ahituv, Shmuel. *Echoes from the Past: Hebrew and Cognate Inscriptions from the Biblical Period*. Jerusalem: Carta, 2008.

Anderson, Gary A. "What about the Canaanites?" Pages 269–82 in *Divine Evil? The Moral Character of the God of Abraham*. Edited by Michael Bergmann, Michael J. Murray, and Michael C. Rea. Oxford: Oxford University Press, 2011.

Assmann, Jan. "Zum Konzept der Fremdheit im alten Ägypten." Pages 77–99 in *Die Begegnung mit dem Fremden: Wertungen und Wirkungen in Hochkulturen vom Altertum bis zur Gegenwart*. Edited by M. Schuster. Colloquium Rauricum 4. Stuttgart: Teubner, 1996.

Avalos, Hector. *Fighting Words: The Origins of Religious Violence*. Amherst, NY: Prometheus, 2005.

Baines, John. "Ancient Egyptian Kingship: Official Forms, Rhetoric, Context." Pages 16–53 in *King and Messiah in Israel and the Ancient Near East: Proceedings of the Oxford Old Testament Seminar*. Edited by John Day. JSOTSup 270. Sheffield: Sheffield Academic, 1998.

Bandy, Alan S. "Vengeance, Wrath and Warfare as Images of Divine Justice in John's Apocalypse." Pages 108–29 in *Holy War in the Bible: Christian Morality and an Old Testament Problem*. Edited by Heath A. Thomas, Jeremy Evans, and Paul Copan. Downers Grove, IL: InterVarsity Press, 2013.

Barker, Dan. *God: The Most Unpleasant Character in All Fiction.* New York: Sterling, 2016.

Bauman, Zygmunt. *Modernity and the Holocaust.* Ithaca, NY: Cornell University Press, 2000.

Beale, G. K. *The Morality of God in the Old Testament.* Christian Answers to Hard Questions. Phillipsburg, NJ: P&R, 2013.

Bergmann, Michael, Michael Murray, and Michael Rea. "Introduction." Pages 1–21 in *Divine Evil? The Moral Character of the God of Abraham.* Edited by Michael Bergmann, Michael Murray, and Michael Rea. Oxford: Oxford University Press, 2011.

Berlejung, Angelika. "Shared Fates: Gaza and Ekron as Examples for the Assyrian Religious Policy in the West." Pages 151–74 in *Iconoclasm and Text Destruction in the Ancient Near East and Beyond.* Edited by Natalie Naomi May. Oriental Institute Seminars 8. Chicago: Oriental Institute, 2012.

Berthelot, Katell. "The Canaanites Who 'Trusted in God': An Original Interpretation of the Fate of the Canaanites in Rabbinic Literature." *JJS* 62 (2011): 233–61.

———. "Where May Canaanites Be Found? Canaanites, Phoenicians, and Others in Jewish Texts from the Hellenistic and Roman Periods." Pages 253–74 in *The Gift of the Land and the Fate of the Canaanites in Jewish Thought.* Edited by Katell Berthelot, Joseph E. David, and Marc Hirshman. Oxford: Oxford University Press, 2014.

Block, Daniel I. *Deuteronomy.* NIVAC. Grand Rapids: Zondervan, 2012.

———. "How Can We Bless You? Wrestling with Divine Violence in Deuteronomy." Pages 31–50 in *Wrestling with the Violence of God: Soundings in the Old Testament.* Edited by M. Daniel Carroll R. and J. Blair Wilgus. BBRSup 10. Winona Lake, IN: Eisenbrauns, 2015.

Boyd, Gregory A. *Crucifixion of the Warrior God: Interpreting the Old Testament's Violent Portraits of God in Light of the Cross.* 2 vols. Minneapolis: Fortress, 2017.

Brehm, Hollie Nyseth. "Re-Examining Risk Factors of Genocide." *Journal of Genocide Research* 19 (2017): 61–87.

Brueggemann, Walter. *Divine Presence Amid Violence: Contextualizing the Book of Joshua.* Eugene, OR: Cascade, 2009.

Bryce, Trevor. *Letters of the Great Kings of the Ancient Near East: The Royal Correspondence of the Late Bronze Age.* London: Routledge, 2003.

Butler, Joshua Ryan. *The Skeletons in God's Closet: The Mercy of Hell, the Surprise of Judgment, the Hope of Holy War.* Nashville: Nelson, 2014.

Caminos, Ricardo A. *Late-Egyptian Miscellanies.* Brown Egyptological Studies 1. London: Oxford University Press, 1954.

Cary, Phillip. "We Are All Rahab Now." *Christianity Today,* July/August 2013, 26–29.

Cave, Alfred A. "Canaanites in a Promised Land: The American Indian and the Providential Theory of Empire." *American Indian Quarterly* 12 (1988): 277–97.

Chalk, Frank, and Kurt Jonassohn. *The History and Sociology of Genocide: Analyses and Case Studies.* New Haven: Yale University Press, 1990.

Charny, Israel. "Toward a Generic Definition of Genocide." Pages 64–94 in *Genocide: Conceptual and Historical Dimensions.* Edited by George J. Andreopoulos. Philadelphia: University of Pennsylvania Press, 1994.

Collins, John J. *Does the Bible Justify Violence?* Facets. Minneapolis: Fortress Press, 2004.

———. "The God of Joshua." *SJOT* 28 (2014): 212–28.

Copan, Paul. *Is God a Moral Monster? Making Sense of the Old Testament God.* Grand Rapids: Baker, 2011.

———. "Yahweh Wars and the Canaanites: Divinely Mandated Genocide or Corporate Capital Punishment? Responses to Critics." *Philosophia Christi* 11 (2009): 73–90.

Copan, Paul, and Matthew Flannagan. *Did God Really Command Genocide? Coming to Terms with the Justice of God.* Grand Rapids: Baker, 2014.

Cowles, C. S. "The Case for Radical Discontinuity." Pages 11–46 in *Show Them No Mercy: Four Views on God and Canaanite Genocide.* Grand Rapids: Zondervan, 2003.

Creach, Jerome F. D. *Violence in Scripture*. Interpretation. Louisville: Westminster John Knox, 2013.

Crossan, John Dominic. *How to Read the Bible and Still Be a Christian: Struggling with Divine Violence from Genesis to Revelation*. New York: HarperOne, 2015.

Crouch, Carly L. *War and Ethics in the Ancient Near East: Military Violence in Light of Cosmology and History*. BZAW 407. Berlin: de Gruyter, 2009.

Cruise, Charles. "A Methodology for Detecting and Mitigating Hyperbole in Matthew 5:38–42." *JETS* 61 (2018): 83–104.

Dallaire, Hélène M. "Taking the Land by Force: Divine Violence in Joshua." Pages 51–74 in *Wrestling with the Violence of God: Soundings in the Old Testament*. Edited by M. Daniel Carroll R. and J. Blair Wilgus. BBRSup 10. Winona Lake, IN: Eisenbrauns, 2015.

David, Joseph E. "Nahmanides on Law, Land, and Otherness." Pages 180–201 in *The Gift of the Land and the Fate of the Canaanites in Jewish Thought*. Edited by Katell Berthelot, Joseph E. David, and Marc Hirshman. Oxford: Oxford University Press, 2014.

Davies, Eryl W. *The Immoral Bible: Approaches to Biblical Ethics*. London: T&T Clark, 2010.

Dawkins, Richard. *The God Delusion*. Boston: Mariner, 2006.

Dossin, Georges. "Une mention de Cananéens dans une lettre de Mari." *Syria* 50.3/4 (1973): 277–82.

Earl, Douglas. "The Christian Significance of Deuteronomy 7." *JTI* 3 (2009): 41–62.

———. "Holy War and חרם: A Biblical Theology of חרם." Pages 152–75 in *Holy War in the Bible: Christian Morality and an Old Testament Problem*. Edited by Heath A. Thomas, Jeremy Evans, and Paul Copan. Downers Grove, IL: InterVarsity Press, 2013.

———. *The Joshua Delusion? Rethinking Genocide in the Bible*. Eugene, OR: Cascade, 2010.

———. *Reading Joshua as Christian Scripture*. JTISup 2. Winona Lake, IN: Eisenbrauns, 2010.

Enns, Peter. *The Bible Tells Me So: Why Defending Scripture Has Made Us Unable to Read It*. New York: HarperOne, 2014.

Fales, Evan. "Satanic Verses: Moral Chaos in the Holy Writ." Pages 91–108 in *Divine Evil? The Moral Character of the God of Abraham*. Edited by Michael Bergmann, Michael J. Murray, and Michael C. Rea. Oxford: Oxford University Press, 2011.

Fenton, Paul. "The Canaanites in Africa: The Origins of the Berbers according to Medieval Muslim and Jewish Authors." Pages 297–310 in *The Gift of the Land and the Fate of the Canaanites in Jewish Thought*. Edited by Katell Berthelot, Joseph E. David, and Marc Hirshman. Oxford: Oxford University Press, 2014.

Filer, Joyce M. "Ancient Egypt and Nubia as a Source of Information for Cranial Injuries." Pages 47–74 in *Material Harm: Archaeological Studies of War and Violence*. Edited by John Carman. Glasgow: Cruithne, 1997.

Fleming, Daniel E. "The Amorites." Pages 1–30 in *The World around the Old Testament*. Edited by Bill T. Arnold and Brent A. Strawn. Grand Rapids: Baker Academic, 2016.

———. *Democracy's Ancient Ancestors: Mari and Early Collective Governance*. Cambridge: Cambridge University Press, 2004.

Flood, Derek. *Disarming Scripture: Cherry-Picking Liberals, Violence-Loving Conservatives, and Why We All Need to Learn to Read the Bible Like Jesus Did*. San Francisco: Metanoia, 2014.

Ford, William A. "The Challenge of the Canaanites." *TynBul* 68 (2017): 161–84.

———. "What about the Gibeonites?" *TynBul* 66 (2015): 197–216.

Fretheim, Terence E. "Violence and the God of the Old Testament." Pages 108–27 in *Encountering Violence in the Bible*. Edited by Markus Zehnder and Hallvard Hagelia. The Bible in the Modern World 55. Sheffield: Sheffield Phoenix, 2013.

Fricker, Miranda. "The Relativism of Blame and Williams' Relativism of Distance." *Proceedings of the Aristotelian Society Supplementary* 84 (2010): 151–77.

Gard, Daniel L. "The Case for Eschatological Continuity." Pages 111–44 in *Show Them No Mercy: Four Views on God and Canaanite Genocide*. Grand Rapids: Zondervan, 2003.

Glassner, J.-J. *Mesopotamian Chronicles*. Edited by Benjamin R. Foster. SBLWAW 19. Atlanta: Society of Biblical Literature, 2004.

Harris, Dana M. "Understanding Images of Violence in the Book of Revelation." Pages 148–64 in *Encountering Violence in the Bible*. Edited by Markus Zehnder and Hallvard Hagelia. The Bible in the Modern World 55. Sheffield: Sheffield Phoenix, 2013.

Hawk, L. Daniel. *The Violence of the Biblical God: Canonical Narrative and Christian Faith*. Grand Rapids: Eerdmans, 2019.

Hays, Richard B. *The Moral Vision of the New Testament: A Contemporary Introduction to New Testament Ethics*. San Francisco: HarperCollins, 1996.

Heimbach, Daniel R. "Crusade in the Old Testament and Today." Pages 179–200 in *Holy War in the Bible: Christian Morality and an Old Testament Problem*. Edited by Heath A. Thomas, Jeremy Evans, and Paul Copan. Downers Grove, IL: InterVarsity Press, 2013.

Heiser, Michael S. *The Unseen Realm: Recovering the Supernatural Worldview of the Bible*. Bellingham, WA: Lexham, 2015.

Hess, Richard S. "'Because of the Wickedness of These Nations' (Deut 9:4–5): The Canaanites—Ethical or Not?" Pages 17–38 in *For Our Good Always: Studies on the Message and Influence of Deuteronomy in Honor of Daniel I. Block*. Edited by Jason S. DeRouchie, Jason Gile, and Kenneth J. Turner. Winona Lake, IN: Eisenbrauns, 2013.

———. "The Jericho and Ai of the Book of Joshua." Pages 33–46 in *Critical Issues in Early Israelite History*. Edited by Richard S. Hess, Gerald A. Klingbeil, and Paul J. Ray, Jr. BBRSup 3. Winona Lake, IN: Eisenbrauns, 2008.

———. *Joshua: An Introduction and Commentary*. Tyndale Old Testament Commentaries. Downers Grove, IL: InterVarsity Press, 1996.

Hoffman, Yair. "The Deuteronomistic Concept of the *Herem*." ZAW 111 (1999): 196–210.

Hofreiter, Christian. *Making Sense of Old Testament Genocide: Christian Interpretations of* Herem *Passages*. Oxford Theology and Religion Monographs. Oxford: Oxford University Press, 2018.

Holloway, Jeph. "The Ethical Dilemma of Holy War." *Southwestern Journal of Theology* 41 (1998): 44–69.

Holloway, Steven W. *Aššur Is King! Aššur Is King! Religion in the Ex-*

ercise of Power in the Neo-Assyrian Empire. CHANE 10. Leiden: Brill, 2002.

Jenkins, Philip. *Laying Down the Sword: Why We Can't Ignore the Bible's Violent Verses*. New York: HarperOne, 2011.

Jones, Adam. *Genocide: A Comprehensive Introduction*. 3rd ed. New York: Routledge, 2017.

Jones, Clay. "We Don't Hate Sin So We Don't Understand What Happened to the Canaanites: An Addendum to 'Divine Genocide' Arguments." *Philosophia Christi* 11 (2009): 53–72.

Kaiser, Walter C., Jr. *Toward Old Testament Ethics*. Grand Rapids: Zondervan, 1983.

Kaminsky, Joel S. *Corporate Responsibility in the Hebrew Bible*. JSOTSup 196. Sheffield: Sheffield Academic, 1995.

Kelle, Brad E. *The Bible and Moral Injury: Reading Scripture Alongside War's Unseen Wounds*. Nashville: Abingdon, 2020.

Kiernan, Ben. *Blood and Soil: A World History of Genocide and Extermination from Sparta to Darfur*. New Haven: Yale University Press, 2009.

Kimball, Dan. *How (Not) to Read the Bible: Making Sense of the Anti-Women, Anti-Science, Pro-Violence, Pro-Slavery and Other Crazy-Sounding Parts of Scripture*. Grand Rapids: Zondervan, 2020.

Kister, Menahem. "The Fate of the Canaanites and the Despoliation of the Egyptians: Polemics among Jews, Pagans, Christians, and Gnostics: Motifs and Motives." Pages 66–111 in *The Gift of the Land and the Fate of the Canaanites in Jewish Thought*. Edited by Katell Berthelot, Joseph E. David, and Marc Hirshman. Oxford: Oxford University Press, 2014.

Kline, Meredith G. "The Intrusion and the Decalogue." *WTJ* 16 (1953): 1–22.

Kuhrt, Amélie. *The Ancient Near East c. 3000–330 BC*. 2 vols. Routledge History of the Ancient World. London: Routledge, 1995.

Lamb, David T. *God Behaving Badly: Is the God of the Old Testament Angry, Sexist and Racist?* Downers Grove, IL: InterVarsity Press, 2011.

Layard, Austen H. *A Second Series of the Monuments of Nineveh Including Bas-Reliefs from the Palace of Sennacherib and Bronzes from the Ruins of Nimroud from Drawings Made on the Spot During a Second Expedition to Assyria*. London: J. Murray, 1853.

Lemkin, Raphaël. *Axis Rule in Occupied Europe: Laws of Occupation, Analysis of Government, and Proposals for Redress*. Washington, DC: Carnegie Endowment for International Peace, 1944.

Lemos, T. M. "Dispossessing Nations: Population Growth, Scarcity, and Genocide in Ancient Israel and Twentieth-Century Rwanda." Pages 27–66 in *Ritual Violence in the Hebrew Bible: New Perspectives*. Edited by Saul M. Olyan. Oxford: Oxford University Press, 2015.

Levene, Mark. *Genocide in the Age of the Nation-State 1: The Meaning of Genocide*. London: Tauris, 2005.

Lieberman, Benjamin. "'Ethnic Cleansing' versus Genocide?" Pages 42–60 in *The Oxford Handbook of Genocide Studies*. Edited by Donald Bloxham and A. Dirk Moses. Oxford: Oxford University Press, 2010.

Lienhard, Joseph T., ed. *Exodus, Leviticus, Numbers, Deuteronomy*. Ancient Christian Commentary on Scripture. Downers Grove, IL: InterVarsity Press, 2001.

Longman, Tremper. "The Case for Spiritual Continuity." Pages 159–90 in *Show Them No Mercy: Four Views on God and Canaanite Genocide*. Grand Rapids: Zondervan, 2003.

Lüdemann, Gerd. *The Unholy in Holy Scripture: The Dark Side of the Bible*. Translated by John Bowden. Louisville: Westminster John Knox, 1997.

MacDonald, Nathan. *Deuteronomy and the Meaning of "Monotheism."* FAT 2:1. Tübingen: Mohr Siebeck, 2003.

Mafico, Temba L. J. "Joshua." Pages 115–19 in *The Africana Bible: Reading Israel's Scriptures from Africa and the African Diaspora*. Edited by Hugh R. Page Jr. Minneapolis: Fortress, 2010.

Masalha, Nur. "Reading the Bible with the Eyes of the Canaanites: Neo-Zionism, Political Theology and the Land Traditions of the Bible (1967 to Gaza 2009)." *Holy Land Studies* 8 (2009): 55–108.

Maul, Stefan M. *Zukunftsbewältigung: Eine Untersuchung altorien-*

talischen Denkens anhand der babylonisch-assyrischen Löserituale (Namburbi). Baghdader Forschungen 18. Mainz: von Zabern, 1994.

Meadors, Gary T., ed. *Four Views on Moving Beyond the Bible to Theology.* Grand Rapids: Zondervan, 2009.

Melville, Sarah C. "Win, Lose, or Draw? Claiming Victory in Battle." Pages 527–37 in *Krieg und Frieden im Alten Vorderasien: 52e Rencontre Assyriologique Internationale International Congress of Assyriology and Near Eastern Archaeology Münster, 17.-21. Juli 2006.* Edited by Hans Neumann, Reinhard Dittmann, Susanne Paulus, Georg Neumann, and Anais Schuster-Brandis. AOAT 401. Münster: Ugarit-Verlag, 2014.

Merrill, Eugene H. "The Case for Moderate Continuity." Pages 61–98 in *Show Them No Mercy: Four Views on God and Canaanite Genocide.* Grand Rapids: Zondervan, 2003.

Moberly, R. W. L. "Election and the Transformation of Ḥērem." Pages 67–89 in *The Call of Abraham: Essays on the Election of Israel in Honor of Jon D. Levenson.* Edited by Gary A. Anderson and Joel S. Kaminsky. Christianity and Judaism in Antiquity 19. Notre Dame: University of Notre Dame Press, 2013.

———. *Old Testament Theology: Reading the Hebrew Bible as Christian Scripture.* Grand Rapids: Baker Academic, 2013.

———. "Toward an Interpretation of the Shema." Pages 124–44 in *Theological Exegesis: Essays in Honor of Brevard S. Childs.* Edited by Christopher Seitz and Kathryn Greene-McCreight. Grand Rapids: Eerdmans, 1999.

Moll, Sebastian. *The Arch-Heretic Marcion.* WUNT 250. Tübingen: Mohr Siebeck, 2010.

Monroe, Lauren A. S. "Israelite, Moabite and Sabaean War-*Herem* Traditions and the Forging of National Identity: Reconsidering the Sabaean Text RES 3945 in Light of Biblical and Moabite Evidence." *VT* 57 (2007): 318–41.

———. *Josiah's Reform and the Dynamics of Defilement: Israelite Rites of Violence and the Making of a Biblical Text.* Oxford: Oxford University Press, 2011.

Monson, John M. "Enter Joshua: The 'Mother of Current Debates' in Biblical Archaeology." Pages 427–58 in *Do Historical Matters Matter to Faith? A Critical Appraisal of Modern and Postmodern Approaches to Scripture*. Edited by James K. Hoffmeier and Dennis R. Magary. Wheaton, IL: Crossway, 2012.

Moran, William L., ed. *The Amarna Letters*. Translated by William L. Moran. Baltimore: Johns Hopkins University Press, 1992.

Morriston, Wes. "Did God Command Genocide? A Challenge to the Biblical Inerrantist." *Philosophia Christi* 11 (2009): 7–26.

Moshman, David. "Conceptions of Genocide and Perceptions of History." Pages 71–92 in *The Historiography of Genocide*. Edited by Dan Stone. Hampshire: Palgrave Macmillan, 2008.

Murphy, Mark C. "God Beyond Justice." Pages 150–67 in *Divine Evil? The Moral Character of the God of Abraham*. Edited by Michael Bergmann, Michael J. Murray, and Michael C. Rea. Oxford: Oxford University Press, 2011.

Niditch, Susan. *War in the Hebrew Bible: A Study in the Ethics of Violence*. New York: Oxford University Press, 1993.

Nielson, Kirsten. "The Violent God of the Old Testament: Reading Strategies and Responsibility." Pages 207–15 in *Encountering Violence in the Bible*. Edited by Markus Zehnder and Hallvard Hagelia. The Bible in the Modern World 55. Sheffield: Sheffield Phoenix, 2013.

O'Brien, Julia M. "Trauma All Around: Pedagogical Reflections on Victimization and Privilege in Theological Responses to Biblical Violence." Pages 185–205 in *La Violencia and the Hebrew Bible*. Edited by Susanne Scholz and Pablo R. Andiñach. Semeia Studies 82. Atlanta: SBL, 2016.

Parkinson, R. B. *Voices from Ancient Egypt: An Anthology of Middle Kingdom Writings*. Oklahoma Series in Classical Culture 9. Norman: University of Oklahoma Press, 1991.

Rainey, Anson F. "Who Is a Canaanite? A Review of the Textual Evidence." *BASOR* 304 (1996): 1–15.

Rainey, Anson F., and R. Steven Notley. *The Sacred Bridge: Carta's Atlas of the Biblical World*. Jerusalem: Carta, 2006.

Räisänen, Heikki. "Marcion." Pages 100–124 in *A Companion to Second-*

Century Christian "Heretics." Edited by Antti Marjanen and Petri Luomanen. VCSup 76. Leiden: Brill, 2005.

Rauser, Randal. "Errant Statements in an Inerrant Book." 19 February 2013. http://randalrauser.com/2013/02/errant-statements-in-an -inerrant-book/.

———. "'Let Nothing That Breathes Remain Alive': On the Problem of Divinely Commanded Genocide." *Philosophia Christi* 11 (2009): 27–41.

Richards, E. Randolph, and Richard James. *Misreading Scripture with Individualist Eyes: Patronage, Honor, and Shame in the Biblical World.* Downers Grove, IL: IVP Academic, 2020.

Römer, Thomas. *Dark God: Cruelty, Sex, and Violence in the Old Testament.* Translated by Sean O'Neill. New York: Paulist, 2013.

Rowlett, Lori L. *Joshua and the Rhetoric of Violence: A New Historicist Analysis.* JSOTSup 226. Sheffield: Sheffield Academic, 1996.

Rowley, Matthew. "The Epistemology of Sacralized Violence in the Exodus and Conquest." *JETS* 57 (2014): 63–84.

Sagi, Avi. "The Punishment of Amalek in Jewish Tradition: Coping with the Moral Problem." Translated by Batya Stein. *HTR* 87 (1994): 323–46.

Sasson, Jack M. *The Military Establishment at Mari.* Studia Pohl 3. Rome: Pontifical Biblical Institute, 1969.

Schmitt, Rüdiger. *Der "Heilige Krieg" im Pentateuch und im deuteronomistischen Geschichtswerk: Studien zur Forschungs-, Rezeptionsund Religionsgeschichte von Krieg und Bann im Alten Testament.* AOAT 381. Münster: Ugarit-Verlag, 2011.

Schwartz, Regina. *The Curse of Cain: The Violent Legacy of Monotheism.* Chicago: University of Chicago Press, 1997.

Seibert, Eric A. *Disturbing Divine Behavior: Troubling Old Testament Images of God.* Minneapolis: Fortress, 2009.

———. "Preaching from Violent Biblical Texts: Helpful Strategies for Addressing Violence in the Old Testament." *Perspectives in Religious Studies* 42 (2015): 247–57.

———. "Recent Research on Divine Violence in the Old Testament (with

Special Attention to Christian Theological Perspectives)." *CBR* 15 (2016): 8–40.

Seitz, Christopher. "Canon and Conquest: The Character of the God of the Hebrew Bible." Pages 292–308 in *Divine Evil? The Moral Character of the God of Abraham*. Edited by Michael Bergmann, Michael J. Murray, and Michael C. Rea. Oxford: Oxford University Press, 2011.

Smith, Mark S. "The Structure of Divinity at Ugarit and Israel: The Case of Anthropomorphic Deities versus Monstrous Divinities." Pages 38–63 in *Text, Artifact, and Image: Revealing Ancient Israelite Religion*. Edited by Gary Beckman and Theodore J. Lewis. BJS 346. Providence, RI: Brown Judaic Studies, 2006.

———. "Ugarit and the Ugaritians." Pages 139–67 in *The World around the Old Testament*. Edited by Bill T. Arnold and Brent A. Strawn. Grand Rapids: Baker, 2016.

Sparks, Kenton L. *Sacred Word, Broken Word: Biblical Authority and the Dark Side of Scripture*. Grand Rapids: Eerdmans, 2012.

Sprinkle, Preston. *Fight: A Christian Case for Non-Violence*. Colorado Springs: Cook, 2013.

Stark, Thom. *The Human Faces of God: What Scripture Reveals When It Gets God Wrong (and Why Inerrancy Tries to Hide It)*. Eugene, OR: Wipf & Stock, 2011.

Stern, Philip D. *The Biblical* Herem: *A Window on Israel's Religious Experience*. BJS 211. Atlanta: Scholars Press, 1991.

Stone, Lawson G. "Early Israel and Its Appearance in Canaan." Pages 127–64 in *Ancient Israel's History: An Introduction to Issues and Sources*. Edited by Bill T. Arnold and Richard S. Hess. Grand Rapids: Baker Academic, 2014.

———. "Ethical and Apologetic Tendencies in the Redaction of the Book of Joshua." *CBQ* 53 (1991): 25–35.

Stump, Eleonore. "The Problem of Evil and the History of Peoples: Think Amalek." Pages 179–97 in *Divine Evil? The Moral Character of the God of Abraham*. Edited by Michael Bergmann, Michael J. Murray, and Michael C. Rea. Oxford: Oxford University Press, 2011.

———. "Reply to Morriston." Pages 204–7 in *Divine Evil? The Moral Character of the God of Abraham*. Edited by Michael Bergmann,

Michael J. Murray, and Michael C. Rea. Oxford: Oxford University Press, 2011.

Suzuki, Yoshihide. "A New Aspect of *Hrm* in Deuteronomy in View of an Assimilation Policy of King Josiah." *Annual of the Japanese Biblical Institute* 21 (1995): 3–27.

Swinburne, Richard. "Reply to Morriston." Pages 232–34 in *Divine Evil? The Moral Character of the God of Abraham*. Edited by Michael Bergmann, Michael J. Murray, and Michael C. Rea. Oxford: Oxford University Press, 2011.

——. "What Does the Old Testament Mean?" Pages 209–25 in *Divine Evil? The Moral Character of the God of Abraham*. Edited by Michael Bergmann, Michael J. Murray, and Michael C. Rea. Oxford: Oxford University Press, 2011.

Tigay, Jeffrey H. *Deuteronomy*. The JPS Torah Commentary. Philadelphia: Jewish Publication Society, 1996.

Tinker, Melvin. *Mass Destruction: Is God Guilty of Genocide?* Welwyn Garden City, UK: Evangelical Press, 2017.

Trimm, Charlie. "Causes of Genocide." Pages 31–49 in *The Cultural History of Genocide*, volume 1: *The Ancient World*. Edited by Tristan Taylor. London: Bloomsbury, 2021.

——. *Fighting for the King and the Gods: A Survey of Warfare in the Ancient Near East*. Resources for Biblical Literature 88. Atlanta: Society of Biblical Literature, 2017.

——. "Recent Research on Warfare in the Old Testament." *CBR* 10 (2012): 1–46.

Troy, Lana. "Religion and Cult during the Time of Thutmose III." Pages 123–82 in *Thutmose III: A New Biography*. Edited by Eric H. Cline and David O'Connor. Ann Arbor: University of Michigan Press, 2006.

Versluis, Arie. *The Command to Exterminate the Canaanites: Deuteronomy 7*. OtSt 71. Leiden: Brill, 2017.

——. "The Early Reception History of the Command to Exterminate the Canaanites." *Biblical Reception* 3 (2014): 308–29.

Walton, John H., and J. Harvey Walton. *The Lost World of the Israelite Conquest: Covenant, Retribution, and the Fate of the Canaanites*. Downers Grove, IL: InterVarsity Press, 2017.

Warrior, Robert Allen. "Canaanites, Cowboys, and Indians: Deliverance, Conquest, and Liberation Theology Today." *Christianity and Crisis* 49 (1989): 261–66.

Weaver, J. Denny. *The Nonviolent God.* Grand Rapids: Eerdmans, 2013.

Webb, William J., and Gordon K. Oeste. *Bloody, Brutal, and Barbaric: Wrestling with Troubling War Texts.* Downers Grove: IVP Academic, 2019.

Weinfeld, Moshe. "The Ban on the Canaanites in the Biblical Codes and Its Historical Development." Pages 142–60 in *History and Traditions of Early Israel: Studies Presented to Eduard Nelson, May 8th, 1993.* Edited by André Lemaire and Benedikt Otzen. VTSup 50. Leiden: Brill, 1993.

Weiss-Wendt, Anton. "When the End Justifies the Means: Raphaël Lemkin and the Shaping of a Popular Discourse on Genocide." *Genocide Studies and Prevention: An International Journal* 13.1 (2019): 173–88.

Wettstein, Howard. "God's Struggles." Pages 321–33 in *Divine Evil? The Moral Character of the God of Abraham.* Edited by Michael Bergmann, Michael J. Murray, and Michael C. Rea. Oxford: Oxford University Press, 2011.

Williams, Stephen N. "Could God Have Commanded the Slaughter of the Canaanites?" *TynBul* 63 (2012): 161–78.

———. "Theological Horizons of Joshua." Pages 93–170 in *Joshua.* Edited by J. Gordon McConville and Stephen N. Williams. Two Horizons. Grand Rapids: Eerdmans, 2010.

Wolterstorff, Nicholas. "Comments on 'What about the Canaanites?'" Pages 283–88 in *Divine Evil? The Moral Character of the God of Abraham.* Edited by Michael Bergmann, Michael J. Murray, and Michael C. Rea. Oxford: Oxford University Press, 2011.

———. "Reading Joshua." Pages 236–56 in *Divine Evil? The Moral Character of the God of Abraham.* Edited by Michael Bergmann, Michael J. Murray, and Michael C. Rea. Oxford: Oxford University Press, 2011.

Wright, Christopher J. H. *The God I Don't Understand: Reflections on Tough Questions of Faith.* Grand Rapids: Zondervan, 2008.

———. "Response to Douglas Earl." Pages 139–48 in *The Joshua Delusion? Rethinking Genocide in the Bible*. By Douglas Earl. Eugene, OR: Cascade, 2010.

Younger, Jr., K. Lawson. *Ancient Conquest Accounts: A Study in Ancient Near Eastern and Biblical History Writing*. JSOTSup 98. Sheffield: JSOT Press, 1990.

———. "Some Recent Discussion on the *Herem*." Pages 505–22 in *Far from Minimal: Celebrating the Work and Influence of Philip R. Davies*. Edited by Duncan Burns and J. W. Rogerson. New York: T&T Clark, 2012.

Zehnder, Markus. "The Annihilation of the Canaanites: Reassessing the Brutality of the Biblical Witnesses." Pages 263–90 in *Encountering Violence in the Bible*. Edited by Markus Zehnder and Hallvard Hagelia. The Bible in the Modern World 55. Sheffield: Sheffield Phoenix, 2013.

INDEX OF AUTHORS

INDEX OF SUBJECTS

INDEX OF SCRIPTURE REFERENCES